W9-ASV-809

"*God,*" Freud wailed, in his most-quoted moment of frustration, "*what do women want?*" Jo Foxworth could *tell him* because she knows—and she can tell you how to get it because she has.

"*Do we really need another book with advice to the managerial woman? The answer is yes,* if it is as lively and informative as this one . . . Women on the way up or hoping to be there would be wise to pick up a copy.★★★★.*"

—*West Coast Review of Books*

"*The name of the book is BOSS LADY, and the author knows what she is talking about* . . . tells how to get there, how to stay there and what to expect on the way. Full of wit, humor and frankness."

—*The Oregonian*

"*Jo Foxworth has made the journey.* She knows every twist and turn . . . and she shares her experience in this amusing and valuable book . . . she has written a telling book . . . her own story plus a 'how-to' manual for women who aim their sights high."

—*Hudson Sun & Marlboro Enterprise*

P.S. "*Men in business should read this one . . .* BOSS LADY is filled with excellent practical suggestions for anyone who wants to make it in business."

—*Detroit Free Press*

ATTENTION: SCHOOLS AND CORPORATIONS

WARNER books are available at quantity discounts with bulk purchase for educational, business, or sales promotional use. For information, please write to: SPECIAL SALES DEPARTMENT, WARNER BOOKS, 666 FIFTH AVENUE, NEW YORK, N.Y 10103.

**ARE THERE WARNER BOOKS
YOU WANT BUT CANNOT FIND IN YOUR LOCAL STORES?**

You can get any WARNER BOOKS title in print. Simply send title and retail price, plus 50¢ per order and 50¢ per copy to cover mailing and handling costs for each book desired. New York State and California residents add applicable sales tax. Enclose check or money order only, no cash please, to: WARNER BOOKS, P.O. BOX 690, NEW YORK, N.Y 10019.

BOSS LADY

Jo Foxworth

An Executive Woman
Talks About Making It

WARNER BOOKS

A Warner Communications Company

WARNER BOOKS EDITION

Copyright © 1978 by Jo Foxworth
All rights reserved. No part of this book may be used or reproduced
in any manner whatsoever without written permission except in the
case of brief quotations embodied in critical articles and reviews.

This Warner Books Edition is published by
arrangement with Thomas Y. Crowell, Publishers.

Cover art by Irving Freeman

Warner Books, Inc.
666 Fifth Avenue
New York, N.Y. 10103

 A Warner Communications Company

Printed in the United States of America

First Warner Books Printing: September, 1979

10

This book is gratefully inscribed to
my agent, Pat Berens, who may have 10 percent
of anything I have any time I have it
. . . and to a couple of friends who are
welcome to split the rest.

Contents

Preface   9

1. Welcome to Boss Land!   11
2. Getting There Is Half the Fun   23
3. Go In to Win   43
4. Packaging Yourself   55
5. More Power to You!   71
6. The Good News and the Bad News: Hiring
   and Firing   81
7. Help! (Working for a Woman)   93
8. "Just a Secretary"   108
9. Shut Up and Listen—You May Learn Something   118
10. Those Little Male Gallantries—Trick or Treat?   130
11. Fellow Travelers   140
12. Drinking Things Over   154
13. The Inquisition   171
14. Going Up the Ladder on Your Back   178
15. Join the Club   188
16. You and Me and the ERA   202
17. Two Against the World   208
18. The Mid-Life Urge   219
19. Your Own Damned Thing   232
20. Where Do We Go From Here?   244
Index   251

Preface

This book has been written on the move, and if that is obvious at times, I'm not really sorry. It was the best I could do. I still had a company to run and clients (thank God!) who expected me to keep working for them, whatever else I might be up to.

It has been written on almost everything that rolls or flies: in Manhattan taxis and the New York Subway system, on buses and commuter trains, on TWA, American and Allegheny Airlines and in a Cessna Skyhawk II while the young pilot was learning to fly it.

The thinking behind it was done partly while staring balefully at Deep Creek Lake in Maryland, partly in restaurants as elegant as Cricket's in Chicago and as plebeian as ZZZ's Coffee Shop around the corner from where I live, but mostly under the bed in my apartment where I tried to sort out my real feelings about being a woman in business and just being a woman. It isn't easy to be either.

Neither is it easy to write a book—particularly one that involves the author's deepest feelings. I have been startled to discover what some of these feelings of mine actually are. Some aren't at all what I thought they were and what I've been saying they were all my life.

This will set the record straight—for me, if for nobody else. In the beginning, however, I did not intend to write a book that reveals so much of myself. The career thrust of women has become a genuine "media event," and it would have been possible to hide behind a slick, professional writing job about it. But the text took over and practically forced me to present things the way I really see them. I may appear to contradict myself, but then life is loaded with contradictions, especially in the business world. And if I make excessive statements, it is because I am an advertising woman, addicted by trade to hyperbole.

I want to thank the people who have helped keep my company alive and those who have helped keep me alive while this was written. They will probably look with wonder upon the lists of dos and don'ts at the end of each chapter. I wish these were a reflection of personal practice because I know, for sure, that they work best for women. But I am capable of violating all of them on any given day, and when I breach even one of them, the cost is painful.

Everybody should have to write at least one book to find out what he or she really thinks, feels, believes. But unless you are a certifiable masochist, I don't recommend it.

1

Welcome to Boss Land!

Boss is a four-letter word, and "Boss Lady" is two of them—double jeopardy and almost a contradiction in terms. The boss is universally depicted as an overbearing, overdemanding *man,* venting his angers and frustrations on suffering underlings who must take it and pretend to love it, whether they like it at all or not. From the avenging God of the Old Testament to Dagwood Bumstead's irascible and unreasonable employer in the comic strips, the boss comes off as an unpredictable male who may strike at any moment with violence and malice.

Back in Mississippi, my father used to get awfully mad at God. Dad was six feet four and an archetypical boss if there ever was one, leading me to suspect that his pique with the deity was mainly a matter of jealousy. He used to rail away by the hour at God's injustice and caprice, criticizing Him in much the same way that he would berate an erratic, soreheaded neighbor.

Who in his right mind, Dad demanded, would order a loyal camp follower like Abraham to murder his first-born son to prove his faith and devotion—and then change his mind after the poor kid had been scared half to death? Who would drown every creature on earth except one very strange family and two each of all the fornicating fauna, just because he didn't like the way everybody else had been acting? And who would turn a member of the surviving family black for laughing at his drunken father's nakedness, because old naked Noah, drunk or sober, was one of God's special favorites?

I knew who. My own dear Daddy would. He would cheerfully do any or all of that and probably could, too, if he put his mind on it. He was that kind of boss. And male down to his heels.

Not so Mr. Dithers, Dagwood's terrible-tempered boss in the funny papers. For all his violence, Mr. Dithers is more than a little tiddly and could never handle power with the flair of God and my father. Still, he communicates the prevailing attitude toward bosses quite handily when he seizes his blundering employee by the throat and chokes him until Dagwood's tongue dangles or beats him over the head and shoulders with a furled umbrella.

Biblical and comic strip excesses discounted, the boss remains a negative entity, suspended somewhere between high awe and low comedy. Nobody wants one. The plain fact is that the boss exercises more control over the lives of his employees and their families than anybody likes to admit—even the boss himself.

In his company's lower and middle echelons he shares a lot of this control—probably more than he wants —with the unions and all levels of government. But way up there in the high-priced seats, where everybody is snapping and clawing to sit, *he* decides: who gets booted down or out and who will be hoisted up the mountain; who gets a salary increase, when and how much; who attends the high-level meetings and in what role; who gets a company car and what kind, who gets a limo with a uniformed driver and who may damned well fight his way to work on the bus or subway; who gets the corner office and the secretary with the British accent; who gets the stock options, use of the private dining room and all the other corporate largess known by the affectionately abbreviated term of "perks."

All these things, of course, affect his employees' whole lifestyles—from where and how they live to whom they socialize with and what their own families, in-laws, neighbors and co-workers think of them. And any boss worth cursing or kissing is troubled by the task of making such life-altering decisions. When Shakespeare wrote, "Uneasy lies the head that wears a crown," he could have been leaving an airport Hilton after having been kept awake by the nightmares of a sheet ripper next door who heads a conglomerate and is on his way to Cleveland to fire one of his vice-presidents.

Some bosses are certifiable sadists, and these are the lucky ones—the ones who can with sincerity and joy hang that sign on the wall reading, "Yea, though I walk through the valley of the shadow of death, I shall fear no evil for I am the meanest sonofabitch in the valley."

Is this any job for a woman?

Tradition says "No." Women have always been the boss behind the boss. Again, the comic strips, which are a continuing social commentary, are loaded with them. And the "bossy wife" sparks the story line in countless novels, plays, short stories and movies of every country. It is a theme so dearly familiar that there can be little doubt that women not only rule the roost but wreak devastating influence on the rooster, far beyond the nesting place. Wives are referred to by their intimidated husbands as "the ball and chain," "the battle-ax," "the warden." And this image of the female helpmate is, of course, the mother lode of material for most of our stand-up comedians—a thought that takes on a certain amount of significance when we are reminded that we laugh loudest at what we fear most. Wives are as uncomfortable about the role as their chagrined husbands.

Unsurprisingly, the boss behind the boss at my own house was Mama. Although Dad was exactly a foot taller and outweighed her by at least a hundred pounds, she never hesitated to dramatize a point by attacking him physically, often with one of the books that she accused him of keeping his nose buried in to avoid talking to her. I remember seeing her assault him once with a novel called *She* by Rider Haggard, for betting $1000 on a heavyweight championship fight. He had come home glowing with bourbon and braggadocio, quite forgetting his promise never to bet more than $1 on anything again— the result of a long losing streak during which Mama had coerced him into taking the pledge. She was doing better with the book than the champ had done with his right cross until Dad told her he had won the bet, whereupon she flung the book aside, took the money away from him and did what any decent recipient of a financial windfall would do. She ran.

Being the boss behind the boss has other rewards, its moments of exhilaration and even glory. Still, there is scant doubt that every woman in the world (well, *almost* every woman) burns to be the boss up front. And the hell with all this make-believe second sexism! The hell with pretending to be brainless and helpless when the pretendee actually is about as brainless as Clare Boothe Luce and as helpless as Muhammad Ali.

Women will joyfully follow a male leader who is genuinely equipped to lead: a man of superior intellect, talent and judgment who knows what he's doing and how it should be done. But the joy perishes when they are expected to knuckle under, at home or at business, to a Neanderthal type whose principal qualification for the job is the accident of gender.

Women who are, themselves, abundantly equipped to lead suffer mightily at being told what to do and how by men who clearly don't know what or how or anything else much except where the men's room and the back doors are located. Usually these women just quietly and surreptitiously perform the task at hand in their own effective way and then have to expend a lot of time and energy perpetrating the illusion that dear Melvin Mediocre is the hero of the day. This not only is malicious waste but is boring and depressing for those being wasted.

I have been a boss of one kind and another for most of my working life, beginning at age twenty-three when I was "advertising manager" of a Mississippi department store. Calling me the advertising manager was euphemism raised to its purest state because there was nothing to manage. I was the entire staff. However, I was the only person around who had a degree from the justly famous School of Journalism at the University of Missouri, and since my major in advertising there indicated that I had some knowledge of the subject, the title pleased all of us: the store owner, his two sons and, most of all, me.

I shared a five-by-eight enclosure with the store's head janitor, an aging black lay preacher who referred to himself always in the third person as Brother Richard. Brother Richard stored his brooms, mops and other implements of office beside and under the long table that held my typewriter, layout board and a pile of newspapers that would have struck envy in the hearts of the Collier brothers. Trying to do creditable advertising under those circumstances was like trying to make love in a telephone booth, and when I was gloomy about it—and that was often—my roommate's evangelical voice would croon, "Brother Richard says wear the world like a loose garment and take Jesus to be your friend."

Occasionally Brother Richard would come back from lunch full of beer and what he called "the Holy Spirit." He would suggest that we pray together, a suggestion I happily accepted because he was an exemplary rhetorician with a prayer. He would pray loudly for us to be delivered from sin, temptation, lust, high living, the evils of money, the deviltry of worldly goods, the "kee-ruption" of power and the hands of the Philistines. I would pray silently to be delivered forthwith into all those wicked and wonderful things. In New York.

I earnestly hope Brother Richard's prayers were answered. Eventually mine were. And I have never once wished I had settled for the black lace lingerie and white boots of "The Total Woman."

If advertising is, indeed, the rat race that it is said to be, I have had the fun of running it on the fastest track there is. I have worked with the best people in the business, fascinating men and women who have given both insanity and nobility new dimensions. And I have seen most of the world the best way of all to see it—for free. Somebody else always footed the bill.

This is a book about how it was and how it is—one woman's view of the problems peculiar to women in business, particularly executive women, who share all the problems of their male counterparts and have to cope with a slew of others which executive men do not face. It is a view based on my own experiences and observations, plus those of women and men I've worked with, talked to and argued with. Needless to say, we don't all agree.

My career is and always has been in advertising, but this book concerns women in other fields, too. That's because advertising is not a business unto itself but performs a service for other businesses. My work in advertising agencies has given me an up-close look at the women who have succeeded or failed—and at this moment are succeeding or failing—in many different fields: food, soft drinks, fashion, cosmetics, liquor, cigarettes, home furnishings, publications, supermarkets and retail stores. It isn't easy for a woman to make it in any of these fields because, no matter what anybody tells you, it's still a man's world. The old, familiar double standard remains on the job full time, perhaps not so overtly as before but in new and subtle forms that are every bit as difficult to overcome.

16

Things Have Changed, But Not Very Much!

At the last reliable nose count, as reported by the Bureau of Labor Statistics in September 1977, there were 37.1 million American women working outside the home in either full-time or part-time jobs. In 1976 alone, the number increased by 1.6 million—almost double the number of new male workers—bringing the total to 48 percent of the adult female population. The majority of these working women, however, are in what *Newsweek* magazine calls "the employment ghetto," doing "women's work" for "women's pay."

In *The Managerial Woman,* the best-selling book by Margaret Hennig and Anne Jardim, it is reported that among workers earning more than $10,000 a year in 1976, fewer than 5 percent were women, and among those earning $25,000 or more, the figure fell to 2.3 percent. This may come as a swift and distinct shock to people who believe that equal opportunity laws and the women's movement have put an end to gender discrimination. It may also boil the blood of young men in large corporations where young women are scrapping it out in tooth-and-nail competition with them now, as never before, for the junior executive jobs. Young white men are beginning to complain now that far from holding the anticipated inside track on employment, they are actually discriminated against in favor of women, black men and that double-threat combination, black women! In New York, Chicago and other large cities the so-called sex wars in business are especially fierce, and while women appear to be making progress in some areas of employment, the situation has not changed as dramatically as we have been led to believe by the media.

The response of business to pressures for equal employment opportunity for women has mainly been at the subbasement level of management, where meaningless titles have been created for the same old jobs. Women who have been working as senior bookkeepers, clerks, computer operators and the like have been christened "managers" or "directing supervisors" and listed on personnel rolls as executives. Their increases in salary, authority and chance for advancement have generally ranged from minimal to zero.

On the other hand, a few large corporations, alarmed by the rumblings from the government and the press, have rushed to ensconce one or two women in top-of-the-mountain jobs with fulsome titles, huge salaries and delicious perks—but no real authority and little chance for advancement. These are the "token women." Like the "token blacks," they are there as window dressing—to display corporate humanism, stave off class-action lawsuits and appease the Feds. They get lovely hush money, status-loaded titles and selected prerogatives of the executive suite, but some of them have nothing more important to do than read the house organ and remind somebody to water the *Dracaena marginata*.

Early last year I phoned a friend who had just been made vice-president in charge of nothing by one of the great image-conscious corporations. I asked how things were going.

"Oh—all right, I guess. It's very nice here," she said, "but weird. I've been here five weeks and still don't have any work to do. This morning I've written a letter to my sister, planned the guest list for a cocktail party and thrown up!"

No wonder she was having nausea attacks. This is a thirty-nine-year-old woman who could run the Third Army, yet the company that is paying her a small fortune has elected to use her simply as a symbol of "enlightened management." A high-salaried, jobless job in a luxurious office may sound like heaven to some people, but my friend doesn't like her sister enough to write her every day, despises cocktail parties and doesn't enjoy throwing up, even in her own private executive bathroom with monogrammed towels and gold-plated fixtures. She is extraordinarily well equipped to make a really meaningful contribution, but that's not what she was hired for.

I am pleased to report that she hung in there, ignoring the fact that she was ignored. She sent suggestion-loaded memos to the men in the upper echelon, she cultivated and impressed the president, and she contributed valuable female-oriented information to this company, whose products happen to be used principally by women. Now she is "semiaccepted," she says—though not quite as a member of the first team.

Such big "jobless jobs" for women may not be common, but it *is* common to put a woman into a showcase spot as a display of corporate social conscience. A female VP I know has a title that creates the impression that she has real clout with the huge soap company she works for. Not so. The man she reports to won't let her sign anything—even a supper slip—unless he's looking over her shoulder. I could quickly name half a dozen others who share similar frustrations.

Another corporate ploy that is used to fog over the appearance of sexism has been the appointment of a highly visible woman to the board of directors. A few women have made careers of being board members, holding three to five directorships at once. Some of them do function in much the same way as the jolly good fellows who sit in the boardroom with them, but a lot of them are, again, "the token women." These female directors are carefully screened, chosen largely from backgrounds that are remote from the kinds of businesses whose boards they are to grace. There is a heavy preference for women who have not been engaged in business per se at all but have worked for nonprofit associations, religious organizations or educational institutions.

I would not be so crass as to suggest that women with backgrounds such as these might be naive about the esoterica of commercial enterprise. After all, the schools, churches and associations have had to haul out the brass knucks and get into some pretty tough fights for survival funds. But Mr. Omnipotence can reasonably expect less flak from them than from a woman who has fought her way up through the ranks of a company like his and knows exactly what he's talking about as he races through the jargon-laden agenda.

So the revolution still rages. And in every revolution, heads must roll. Thousands have already gone up on the pikes, male heads among them. This is particularly true in companies where woman are taking aim at the real power jobs. A few—depressingly few—are getting them. Some others are getting their heads sheared off just below their $500 wigs and Kenneth hairdos. And there are unsuspecting men bumbling into the same bloody fate as part of the scenario for revolt.

Women are getting booted out of good jobs or the opportunity to get better ones because Somebody Up There thinks they're "pushing too hard." Men are experiencing the same misfortune because Somebody Up There decides they're not opening the doors to women wide enough, fast enough. And whole corporations, still chafing over racial quotas, are getting zapped by government and the courts for dragging their feet on equal employment opportunity for women.

In the advertising business, where we live and die by statistics on purchasing power and consumer demand, there is general agreement that women buy up to 80 percent of all the consumer goods and services sold in America. Yet these goods and services are almost 100 percent designed by men, made by men and, except at the bottom level of retailing, sold by men. Leaving out the whole matter of "rights," equality and fairness, isn't there something basically wrong with this picture?

The men who perpetuate this practice justify it on grounds that they get extensive "input" from women via market research, unquestionably a valid and valuable aid. But the same men cheerfully admit that nine out of ten new products introduced each year on the supermarket shelves fail and disappear within a few weeks. Question: Couldn't the track record be improved with active participation in product development by the sex that does the buying?

The logic behind a lot of our current product design, development and packaging escapes me. I don't believe any woman in her right mind would ever have invented the blister pack—the plastic "bubble" that seals thousands of products onto a display card. A principal function of the blister pack is to frustrate shoplifters, but the person it frustrates most is the purchaser. It defies all effort to get at the merchandise inside without using a hacksaw or destroying a whole manicure and half of one's fingernails. Similarly, I can see no reason why men should design and oversee production of almost all the products a woman uses—from brassieres to refrigerators and stoves. While I do not believe it is necessary to be a woman in order to produce acceptable products for women, neither do I believe that it is necessary to be a man.

Business does need women—not as surrogate men but as what they are: female people with another dimension of intellect, knowledge and experience. These qualities can and should be put to work at all corporate levels to improve not only that vaunted "bottom line" but the acceptability of the products offered for sale.

If you're a woman entertaining ideas about becoming a Boss Lady, here are some broad guidelines:

1. *Be sure that a business career is what you really want.* It's not for everybody (even all the men), and if something deep inside you keeps saying, "Not me," feel free to stay home. You can find ways to earn money there if you need it—and fulfilling things to do besides housekeeping and child care. (The inventor of the Jonny Mop was Dorothy Rodgers, wife of the famous Broadway musical composer Richard Rodgers; she didn't need the $2 million she got for the invention but did enjoy the achievement.) Remember that while 48 percent of the women are working outside the home, 52 percent still are not.

2. *Find a company whose principles you agree with and whose principals you respect.* It's tough to be holed up with thieves unless you have a penchant for larceny yourself—no fun, in fact, to be with any organization whose attitudes and ethics don't match yours. Work for people you can be loyal to out of sincere admiration, and if you discover you can't be loyal to them, quit.

3. *Be friendly and pleasant to everybody.* "Today's mailroom clerk may be tomorrow's president" is a much quoted cliché because it's true. So is the reverse, which produced that other little homily: "Be nice to the people you meet going up because you're likely to meet them again coming down."

4. *Put on a happy face.* Business rides on confidence, courage and optimism. The people at the top are getting enough bad news already without having to wonder what else has gone wrong. Few things are more welcome around an office than an "up" appearance, so smile! It's an instant face-lift. And a free one.

5. *Don't try to make the people around you forget you're a woman—and don't forget it yourself.* It may be one of your strongest assets. Business doesn't need make-believe men. It needs skillful, confident people of both sexes, and you shouldn't have to change yours to succeed.

22

2

Getting There Is Half the Fun

As we've already seen, if the birth accident you experienced caused you to be born female, getting your share of the goodies in business or anywhere else isn't going to be easy. Few women, even the fabled high rollers who always seem to get what they want, will deny that it's still a man's world. But that doesn't mean you can't make it. You *can* get what you want, but first of all, you have to *know what that is*—and how much you really want it.

I guess I always knew I wanted to be in the advertising business. I learned to read on the Campbell's Soup ads, following their classic typography with a chubby finger that often streaked the pages with chocolate ice cream. I was enchanted with those Campbell kids in the magazine ads and, interestingly, never dreamed of having a pair like them for my very own. I only burned to write the simpleminded quatrains printed under their pictures.

Maybe you're not blessed—or should I say cursed? —with such a strong career direction. But in any event, don't approach the so-called job market undecided and uncommitted. It's the surest way to remain unemployed or, what is worse, ungainfully tied up. I talk to an astonishing number of young women who want a job but don't have the dimmest idea about the kind of work they'd like to do. They do, however, express a strong interest in making money—and a high regard for the business world that would have been repugnant to their age group in the 1960s and early 1970s.

Geraldine Rhoads, the distinguished editor-in-chief

of *Woman's Day,* has some significant insights into this resurgence of respect for business. Distributed through all the nation's major supermarkets, *Woman's Day* has an estimated readership of nineteen million (mostly female), and the readers' letters that pour into the magazine's offices each week provide a fascinating cross section of current opinion. Speaking at a New York meeting of the National Council of Women, Editor Rhoads said this:

> We've been through some important changes in women's objectives . . . especially toward money.
>
> Even the women who vehemently denied being feminists agreed, early on, that "equal pay for equal work" seemed only fair.
>
> Now they want financial recognition for the housewife—new benefits respecting her economic contribution.
>
> There was a time, of course, when it was hard to justify raises for many young women: they were so clearly just marking time, before marriage or children. Now a great many want to know what sort of career path lies before them.
>
> Even in my business, which inevitably attracts a large proportion of the women with literary interests, or a bent for social service, there are important changes in attitudes. Our readers, job applicants, staffers, college women touching base for career advice—all have new definitions of success. They want to grow, they want to make money, and often they see *business* or the *business side* (of a publishing operation like ours) as the arena they will choose for getting ahead, and making things happen. This last is especially true of the younger women, who are busily plotting their lives. They're a new breed of idealists—seeing themselves as creative and socially effective people with a new clout they expect to derive from the MBA's they're taking as adjuncts to their other studies. And they do expect to be paid

salaries commensurate with their contribution to the business.

This attitude toward business and money represents, to me, a refreshing change—and a recognition that the philosophy of helping people does not begin and end in social work. Since business ultimately underwrites everything, including the social services, it may be assumed that virtually all legitimate business activity helps some people in some way. This assumption should broaden the scope of career choices for the idealistic and, at the same time, make selection all the more difficult. And another factor further complicating the choice is the opening up of fields that used to be closed to women.

Women may now be employed to do so-called men's jobs and, under the law, *must* be hired for this work if they are qualified and insist on having them. Of course, an employer who is determined to hold the gender line can find ways to circumvent the law, and resentful male employees can make female "interlopers" uncomfortable enough to quit. Still, there are women at work today in scores of jobs that until recently were the exclusive domain of men: as steelworkers, telephone linepersons, jockeys, police officers, oilfield workers and coal miners— this last, in spite of the old superstition that the presence of a woman in a coal mine, for any reason, is the worst kind of bad luck.

There are lots of female cab drivers and bus drivers, too, although many a man makes a habit of passing up these female-driven vehicles, stating simply and sincerely that he'd rather walk. (Incidentally, the jokes that women detest most are the ever-present ones that ridicule their capabilities as drivers. Small wonder, since recent statistics of the National Safety Council show that in ten million miles of driving by both sexes, women have almost 14 percent fewer accidents.)

25

A woman cab driver in New York told me that she always gets her pick of the taxis. "You see," she said, "a cab driver is the boss of that taxi while it's on the streets, and the fleet owner knows I'm going to baby any car I'm driving. You know, take good care of it and drive carefully. In eight years of fighting New York traffic, I've never had an accident!" At the other end of the country, in Jackson, Mississippi, the owner of the city's largest limo and taxi fleet is a woman—Flora Schaufler. Ms. Schaufler employs drivers of both sexes and says she wishes she could find more woman drivers because "they treat the cars and the passengers better."

Liberation Begins at Home—Like Charity

I am not surprised to see women excelling at male-oriented activities. Although I have never been a sign-carrying member of the women's liberation movement, I am, indeed, a liberated woman and have been since puberty. It would be gratifying if I could cite this as grand-scale personal achievement, but candor compels me to admit it was a simple matter of geography: I was born and reared in Mississippi, where the choice was between early liberation and more or less permanent pregnancy. I decided it would be more comfortable as well as more interesting to be free.

My birthplace was a town called Tylertown, population 1102. An overromantic schoolteacher of mine once described it as "a sleepy little village that hangs on the highway like a bead on a rosary." Recent upswings in the economy down South may have made the description more fitting now. But in those days Tylertown hung on the highway in a cloud of red dust and cotton lint, gasping for breath and usually praying for rain to cool things off.

Like most of the career women I know, I grew up under the spell of a colorful father. Dad was in what might be courteously termed "the restaurant business." He hadn't intended to be. Actually he hadn't intended to be in any business at all, having been born into what he called "broken-down Southern aristocracy," a band of dreamers whose only ambition was to get by without working. Until he was twenty-six, he got by on the proceeds from minor gambling. All he really liked to do was read, fish, hunt and shoot pool.

It was the pool shooting that changed his life, landing him in a commercial undertaking he denounced as a time waster that he had no taste, aptitude or patience for. One Saturday afternoon, when he was playing for blood and money in the local billiards parlor, he blazed through an incredible winning streak that he always recalled as "the worst misfortune of my life." He won the pool hall. It was a misfortune because the woman he loved (who was to become my mother) refused to marry a man who owned a pool hall. The best he could do to appease her was swap it for the restaurant next door.

Dad's restaurant would have made a magnificent stage set for *The Ballad of the Sad Café*. One side was furnished with six cloth-covered tables set under artificial potted palms for gracious dining. The other side was equipped with a counter faced by twelve wobbly, spin-around stools. At one end of the counter stood a cold drink bin stocked with Coca-Cola, Nehi and a bright-green lemon-flavored drink made locally by an entrepreneur known as "Pop" Ellzey. At the other end of the counter was a cigar case, the cash register and Dad.

Three ceiling fans creaked and whined through the long, hot days, stirring the steamed-up air and reddish dust. Shorty Owens, who did all the work while Dad sat at the cash register reading, rushed around lamenting that he was too tall to be a midget and too short to be a man.

Dad died when I was nine and he was thirty-nine—of stubbornness. He had an attack of appendicitis when he was on a fishing outing with cronies, and he wouldn't stop rowing the boat. Because he had lost the toss that day, it was his turn to row, and he saw the commitment through. By the time he got back to town the available medical practice of the day could not save his life.

Mama was left with two children, a broken-down restaurant and $5000 worth of life insurance, much of which she spent burying Dad in the majestic manner his family expected. She determined to educate my sister and me via the restaurant, and with the help of her sister (my beloved Aunt Freda), she did.

My best friends were Tee and Elee, twin girls with perfect coordination and four sports-minded brothers, a combination that made them red-hot swimmers, golfers, tennis players, basketball dribblers, pitchers, catchers, fielders, base stealers, and homerun hitters. (Years later, when Tee's son was having trouble with his pitching in the Little League, she took him to an isolated spot, where they swore each other to secrecy, after which she taught him how to pitch curves with a softball.)

I was a physical moron. I had no coordination, no brothers and fifteen pounds of excess "baby fat" that were no help on the playing fields or anywhere else. My only salvation was to excel in nonphysical things, which are largely unacceptable alternatives to children. The unhappy result was that I became a smart-ass kid. If I had been born in the Bronx, I might have become another Bella Abzug—who would probably be the first to admit that one Bella Abzug in the world is quite enough. I don't know about Bella, but a lot of female overachievers I do know about were overweight little girls. In this golden age of amateur psychiatry the link needs no belaboring.

Champs that they were, Tee and Elee could easily afford to conceal their intellect, and did. Also, they never let me get too far out of line with my own miserably elected smart-assery. I can't recall that they ever beat me up, but there was always the off chance that they would. I saw the frontier-style justice they regularly pummeled out to the town bully, who was four years older and more than a head taller than they were. He couldn't bear the humiliation of having been vanquished in a schoolyard fist-fight by mere girls, even two of them. He kept coming back to reopen hostilities, hoping to prove that their previous victories were flukes, the result of a few lucky punches. But the "lucky punches" kept landing, and seeing the damage they did to the toughest kid in the county, I learned some valuable lessons in restraint.

In high school I stared out the window a lot, dreaming of worlds "out there" to invade, if not to conquer, and composing shaky quatrains about lost love, death and Campbell's Soup. After school and during the summer vacations I worked for the local weekly newspaper. I wrote some heavy "think pieces" for the Tylertown *Times* and a few adolescent imitations of satire for *The Black & Gold,* our high school newspaper, which was edited by Vic Roby, now an announcer for NBC-Television.

The Low Side of Higher Education

With Tee and Elee, I enrolled in Mississippi State College for Women, known sequentially as Messy W, The W, and MUW—the latter because in 1974 it became Mississippi University for Women. Although I enjoyed the general arts courses offered there, I was unhappy that the college offered no special training in advertising and journalism and made myself unpopular in the administration offices with a continuing harangue about this. I suspect that the administration, dependent as it was on the state legislature for funds, felt that it was more circumspect to train students to be planters' wives than businesswomen.

I further distinguished myself at The W by flunking all the gym courses, and in fact, I may be the only woman in the school's ninety-three-year history who flunked a gym course called "Rest-in-the-Room." Enrolling me in that one was a last-resort effort of the Physical Education Department to find something I could get a passing grade on. The effort bombed when I was caught socializing in a campus hangout called The Goose during the time when I was supposed to be resting in my room. That cooked my goose in phys. ed. forever.

After three years of literature, history, music appreciation, art appreciation, zoology and such I migrated to the University of Missouri to major in advertising at the School of Journalism there. From what I have heard and read of boot camp, I can only believe that my Jay School teachers were all onetime drill sergeants in the Marine Corps. After going through their scholastic obstacle courses, everything I have been called upon to do since then has seemed idiotically easy.

The best advertising courses were taught by E. K. Johnston, who had the disposition of a stepped-on snake. E. K. was small, dapper, red-haired, brilliant and hellbent on stamping out undergraduate ignorance. He would explode through the swinging doors of the lecture hall, shouting at machine-gun pace, spraying the area with facts, figures and deadly accurate observations.

I learned a lot about the advertising business at the University of Missouri, including the basics of most skills that are associated with it. My training there has equipped me to know what may be reasonably expected of other people on a "normal" timetable or in an emergency situation. This is an especially valuable skill for a Boss Lady, for whom one of the most important things is to be able to avoid the "unreasonable" label.

The University of Missouri School of Journalism not only publishes a daily newspaper but operates a radio and television station as serious business enterprises. This permits students to learn by doing all the jobs associated with the curriculum, giving them an authentic baptism by fire. We had to do legwork as reporters, write news and feature stories, write headlines, edit releases that came off the Associated Press wire, make engravings, shoot pictures and set type—all with no compensation.

We also had to sell advertising to the local merchants. I can remember hoping fervently that nobody would buy an ad because if that happened, I'd have to write it, lay it out, somehow get it illustrated and then set it up.

I picked up a lot of other valuable information, too. Among other things I learned how to drink out of a jug, an over-the-shoulder bit of finesse that came in handy years later when I wrote copy for a distillery. This bit of esoteric knowledge impressed a group of liquor executives who until that moment had resisted the idea of involving a woman in their business, a veritable male bastion. It should be emphasized, however, that I did not *demonstrate* the jug ploy. I only wrote about it. A demonstration might have stirred up some classic male fears. Men often complain that woman do things to destroy their "vision of womanhood," and although drinking out of a jug slung over the shoulder can be an amusing bit, I had a strong suspicion that this might be one of those vision-shattering acts.

I also learned how to time an exit from a nightclub disturbance so as to see the best of the fight without being on the premises when the police arrived to arrest everybody. A Boss Lady or a young woman who expects to be one should never be trapped in a situation that could result in unfavorable publicity for herself or her firm.

At the University of Missouri I was also taught the

value of being on time, which is even more important to women than men because the female sex is the one with the reputation for always being late. (Never mind the reality; that's the reputation!) Lessons in on-timesmanship were served up as a side dish by Roscoe Ellard, who subjected me to the torture of humiliation in the presence of my peers. His class in advertising principles and practices met at 8 A.M. on Mondays, Wednesdays and Fridays. I had no problem with eight o'clock on Tuesdays and Thursdays, when I was dazzlingly punctual for my classes. But on Mondays, Wednesdays and Fridays, Freud and the devil took over. No matter how hard I tried to get to Dr. Ellard's high-minded lecture on time, I was always four or five minutes late. It drove him crazy, and he made me suffer for it.

The professor and I did not love each other anyway. He had a loathing for my Southern accent so intense that I suspect he connected it in some way to his own speech impediment, a choking hang-up that suspended a sentence in midair until the offending word finally exploded in a high-pitched shout. When he asked me a question, he would explain to the class that he thought it might be amusing to get "a dialectical reply with a r-r-rrrrrrrr-REGIONAL viewpoint."

It was not possible to get into the lecture hall unobserved, for it could be entered only through the swinging doors that flanked the lecture platform. My seat was in the fifth row, center, and there was no way I could sneak into it without Dr. Ellard's seeing me. He waited for me. The eminent professor stood at the lectern, staring silently at the class, until I rushed miserably into the hall. He would jump from the platform, offer me his arm with the formality of an usher at a church wedding and escort me to the row where I sat. After seating me, he would ask if he could get me anything. "Coffee, Or-r-rrrrrrrr-

ORANGE juice?" The class tittered, and I grew old and died of embarrassment at least twenty times that semester before I finally managed to arrive on time. Since then I have almost never been late for a business appointment, and I want to thank Dr. Ellard now, wherever he is, although gratitude was no part of what I felt at the time.

It's Easier Now. Or at Least, It *Looks* Easier.

Today's colleges and universities, Mississippi University for Women and the University of Missouri among them, offer hundreds of exciting new career opportunities to women. There are so many women now enrolled in the nation's law schools that the young men protest that they are being crowded out. There are also scores of young women approaching the job market armed with MBA degrees, a rare thing for a woman even five years ago. And hundreds more who are studying such supposedly "unfeminine" subjects as engineering, criminology, divinity, politics and veterinary medicine. According to the American Veterinary Medicine Association, as of September 1, 1977, there were 1,993 women practicing the science—including a scattering of specialists in large animals such as horses, cows and zoo creatures—an increase of a little more than 46 percent since 1972.

Whereas women used to be considered adorable dummies in math, they are now rushing into specialties involving sophisticated computer techniques and such advanced classics as calculus. A particular increase has been noted in the number of female CPAs, who seem to like the idea of setting up their businesses and becoming Boss Ladies fresh out of college. And at the mature end of the spectrum, June Thursh, who opted for early retirement from the J. C. Penney Co., at the beginning of

1978 is forming the first insurance underwriting firm for women, a new kind of insurance business that will be devoted to "total financial planning" for women.

Educational institutions, by and large, are showing accelerated interest in women's studies, with special workshops exploring career options, female adjustment, female revolt and contemporary issues in feminist psychology. There are also courses available on female sexuality, examining the cultural, historical and social sources that have shaped it. This new interest in the education of women for meaningful roles in an aware society is a refreshing switch.

Making It from Mississippi to Manhattan

My first job was in McComb, Mississippi, a town that is more widely known for the ugliness of past racial problems than for the beauty of its continuing azalea festival. I worked for the McComb *Daily Enterprise,* a newspaper edited and published by Oliver Emmerich, one of the grand "firebrand" editors that the South seems to spawn more readily than any other region. His wife, Lyda Will, is a delightful woman given to hiding a first-class mind behind the old Southern custom of appearing "scatter-brained." Although she didn't come into the office often, she was unquestionably the Boss Lady behind the boss and Oliver's equal in management whenever she wanted to be.

I will always remember how Lyda Will settled a rape case involving an *Enterprise* employee. Every woman knows that rape is no laughing matter. But sexual morality, or lack of it, sometimes is. On this occasion a printer who worked at the *Enterprise* was accused of rape by a woman who had lived with him for ten years. Learning that this was an authentic lover's quarrel, Lyda

Will set out to shortcut the difficulties. She knew that the printer's father was a pig farmer who always had a smokehouse full of hams, bacon and sausage. So Lyda Will persuaded the woman to drop the rape charge for the following considerations: one ham, a side of bacon, five pounds of sausage and $10 in cash. It was cheaper than legal fees for the accused, and the settlement saved Oliver Emmerich the aggravation of getting a temporary replacement for a valued employee. Everybody was so happy with the outcome that the feuding couple promptly went back together.

I had been hired to sell and write advertising at the *Enterprise,* but I cheerfully made a nuisance of myself by insisting on doing some of everything involved in getting out a daily newspaper. I had learned the basics at the University of Missouri and set about extending them. Having always been something of a dilettante, I like doing a lot of different things, and at the *Enterprise* I had the opportunity. I watched Oliver Emmerich and his managing editor O. C. McDavid, very closely, listened to every word they said and read every word they wrote. Joe Cantlon and Eddie Myers grudgingly showed me how to set type on the Ludlow machine, and Johnny Williams, the handsome mulatto pressman, let me watch him thread the ancient flatbed presses with newsprint. This is a complicated process, and a passing acquaintance with it has made it possible for me to appear to know more about printing than I actually do.

All the News That Was Unfit to Print!

I was also permitted to edit some of the Associated Press news, write some front-page headlines and some of the rich, beautiful prose that went on the society page. Part of my education there was learning how to handle an enraged matron whose daughter's wedding dress had been described with seven words fewer than had been used for the candlelight satin creation worn by the daughter of a woman she hated. I also learned to check the copy sent in by the rural correspondents very carefully. One of them was particularly creative in sending items about people she wanted to spite:

"Mr. and Mrs. Elton Ginsberry are announcing the birth of a 19-pound son."

"Mr. Clive Morris is back in the hospital. Doctors will not say what is wrong but it is felt that he will be up and around again in the usual five days it takes to get him back on his feet."

"Miss Ruth Fletcher is engaged again, this time to a man from Bogalusa. Everyone wishes her luck."

After a year at the *Enterprise* I started looking for a job that would increase my poverty-line income and learned that opportunities were opening up for women in retailing. I found this to be the case at Kennington's, "Mississippi's Largest Department Store," where *père* Kennington and his two sons respected the capabilities of women and placed them in key jobs as a matter of policy. (Actually retailers have long been ahead of the pack in this way.) The Kenningtons taught me the retail business —which is actually the crucial point of just about everybody's business and, therefore, valuable beyond any accounting. They sent me to the markets in New York, Chicago and Los Angeles with buyers and, in spite of my youth, permitted me to take the initiative in working out master promotion strategy with merchandising managers and the resident buying office in Manhattan.

At Kennington's (now a store in the burgeoning McRae's chain) I planned promotion themes for the store at large and for individual departments, scheduling the advertising and the window displays that supported them. I was also responsible for creating and "placing" the advertising—that is, putting it together and getting it to the various media on some pretty impossible deadlines. Working with most store buyers is no barrel of laughs. They are tense people who are usually involved in fashioning nooses for their necks which will be drawn tight at the same time next year—that is, they are expected to "beat" whatever figures they recorded each day of the previous year—and that doesn't make them easy to get along with. They fight for advertising space and display windows, and having to deny either to a desperate man or woman is a job for the Marine Corps. Three of the people hired to help me saved my sanity. They were an artist named Colleen Nordin and two copywriters from Missouri named Suzanne Sames and Suzanne Bassford.

The two Suzannes were charmed with Mississippi, never more so than on a day when, as we were checking the display windows, we were approached by a farmer who wanted to know about a sweater on one of the mannequins.

"You ladies work here?" he asked.

"Yes, we do," I said.

"Tell me," he said, "what will you take for that sweater on that statue standing there?"

"Ninety dollars," I said. "It's a very fine cashmere."

"Yea, but is that a warm sweater?" he asked.

"Very warm," I said.

"Okay," he replied. "Get it out of that window for me. My wife wants a sweater to milk the cow in!"

Oil had been discovered on the farmer's "dirt farm," and he soon became a spectacular customer of the store. Please note, however, that although he bought his wife a $90 cashmere sweater, she was still expected to milk the cow.

I adored "The Store" and the Kenningtons, but I had not been converted to Brother Richard's attitude toward the evil that lurked in the world beyond our broom closet. Eventually, a large salary increase lured me to a store in Louisville, Kentucky, where I became advertising and sales promotion director.

There were three great things about Louisville: Churchill Downs, the mahogany bar in the Brown Hotel, where the definitive mint julep was served, and a tree at the bend of a road through Cherokee Park. Unfortunately I could not spend much time at the races, at the bar or under the tree. Most of my days were squandered gazing up at the lofty eminence of Norbert Fallone, the pompous store president who sat at a desk on top of a very high platform. Mr. Fallone did not affect this elevation because he was small. He was, in fact, six feet two inches. I think he did it because he *felt* small, and that is the kind of man a businesswoman should avoid at all cost.

I didn't know about the raised desk when I took the job because my interview with Fallone had taken place in New York. This was a mistake I never repeated. Since then I have made a practice of talking to men (and women) in their natural work habitats before agreeing to become associated with them. Most people behave differently in different settings. Certainly Mr. Fallone was not the same man in Louisville I had met in New York.

It was a bad scene but I played it for four months. I resigned the day he called me a prima donna—and mispronounced it. Even in Tylertown, we knew it was "prē-ma-dŏn'-a," and I could never stand being called names by people who can't pronounce them.

At this point in my life I went home to think things over. My mother and Aunt Freda, who were very close, were by then living in Louisiana and I joined them there to do some stocktaking, examine my options and decide where to go from there. I did a lot of this while fishing in the bayous with my aunt. I knew that I was equipped by talent, training and experience to handle an important job. But where? Although I had a lot to offer, nothing much was being offered in return. My mother didn't want me to leave the South, and twenty years ago opportunities in advertising were very limited there. Opportunities for women were even more so—and still are, North, South, East and West.

When I finished thinking things over, I got up and headed East. I first landed in the place where W. C. Fields said "on the whole" he'd rather be than dead: Philadelphia. I never understood Fields' continuing put-down of Philly or any of the other jokes about its dullness that are standard with amateur and professional comedians. To me, it is a charming city, full of delightful crazy people. Because there's not much excitement around town, like Mississippians, they create their own.

There was plenty of excitement in the store where I worked. It was one of the last citadels of "high fashion," and it was patronized by the rich, the foolish and the ambitious-foolish who wanted to appear rich. One customer habitually threw her $20,000 sable coat onto the floor for her dogs to doze on while she shopped. Another bought four extremely sexy black cocktail dresses because she was in mourning for her recently deceased husband. Still a third would come in and buy "all the size fourteens" because she didn't have time to try on anything—and never returned one of them. We sold mink ice buckets, lucite toothbrushes and diamond-studded ID tags for dogs and cats priced at $160.

The firm was headed by a woman whom I'll call Lori Pushkin. She taught me more than I ever wanted to know about snob appeal. "People will buy anything," she said, "and pay anything for it, if they think it's going to make the right impression on the right person at the right time." My observations since then have convinced me that she knew what she was talking about.

After a year at the Pushkin salon, I decided to tackle

the area of advertising known as Madison Avenue. I was assured by everybody who knew anything about it that I was unemployable by a New York advertising agency. Everybody except a copywriter named Joan Chamberlain. According to the Cassandras, I had two strikes against me which added up to three First, I had no advertising experience of any kind in New York. Secondly (and thirdly), I had no advertising *agency* experience anywhere.

I preferred to believe Joan Chamberlain. Since my only experience had been in retail advertising, I had no samples of national advertising to prove or even indicate my ability to do it. So I set about making some up. I wrote campaigns for coffee. automobiles, cake mixes, banks, beer, electrical appliances and insurance companies. I invented new products and named them. I created new packaging ideas. I made phone calls, wrote letters and talked to anybody I could get in to see on Madison Avenue. I got doors slammed in my face, got advised (sometimes sympathetically, sometimes sarcastically) to go back to Mississippi and got wet every day because it rained that entire spring. I also, at last, got a job. I wasn't making a living wage, but I was where I had set out to be: in a real, live advertising agency. On Madison Avenue!

Since then I have met, observed and talked with women in every kind of business there is. All of them, of course, have different career histories, and there is disagreement among them as to how a young woman today should approach the job market. They all agree on one point, however: getting where you want to be isn't easy, but if you like the kind of work you're doing, getting there is half the fun. Here are my own suggestions:

1. *Choose a field you really enjoy—not one that happens to be "in" at the moment.* This year's big "ins" can be next year's big "outs," leaving you in an area you

can't stand after the bright promise has gone over the rainbow. Don't pick a field because it's what a friend or lover or dear old Dad is doing, and don't try to follow in somebody's footsteps if your feet don't fit them. Women tend to ask men for career advice, and men tend to advise them to do something "feminine." If you prefer a field that the men in your life find unbecoming, pay no attention. Genuinely liking what you do means you're apt to be very good at it, and that makes it all the more likely for you to reap tangible rewards.

2. *Get the specialized training you need for the field.* Men do this automatically, and so should you. You, of course, know that no amount of education can guarantee your success, and you know also that there are dozens of stoics who've made it without any formal education at all. However, as technology advances, possibilities grow dimmer for the gifted "primitives." Equipping yourself with special knowledge and skills in your chosen field gives you a head start. It also indicates to any skeptics around you that you're serious about the business.

3. *When you get a job, learn everything you can about it and every other job that touches it.* Getting into a field usually requires you to be a specialist, but getting to be a boss always requires that you be a generalist. If you aspire to be Boss Lady in the company, get the overall qualifications you need.

4. *Don't be a grasshopper about your career.* Grasshoppers know they're going to jump but not where they're going to land. Work out a plan based on the length of time you expect to work (all your life, X number of years) and what you want to accomplish. Women are more inclined to leave things to chance, and they've only been serious contenders in the job market for a few years. Don't be discouraged if the plan doesn't go according to schedule. Business plans seldom do, but think what a shambles your life will be if you have no plan at all.

5. *Do not, under any circumstances, work for a man who puts his desk on a platform.* A man who does this is difficult for anybody to make points with—and impossible for women.

6. *When you've made a mistake in a job choice, admit it.* And correct it as quickly as you can. Things aren't always the way they seem in the glow of an interview, and they sometimes *are* misrepresented. If it develops that the chemistry between you and your employer is really wrong, the situation is less likely to be productive than explosive. Get out before the blowup. A woman will often hang onto a mistake, feeling that it's somehow her fault because she's been conditioned to "face the blame." Don't.

7. *Take time out to examine your options and think things over when you need to.* You can't afford it? You can't afford not to! It's your life that's affected. And if you've chosen to follow a career, it should be as important to you as it is to any man.

8. *Whatever you decide to do, do not believe the people who tell you you can't do it.* If you want it badly enough, you can find a way. The fact that you're "just a girl" doesn't really matter unless you let it.

3

Go In to Win

How does a woman get to be a Boss Lady? And why is the achievement still so novel and strange that this remains the question most often asked of every Boss Lady in the world? Put another way, why do women of superior capabilities remain stuck in nothing-type jobs, while men with mediocre qualifications sail over their heads and into the executive suite?

One entirely significant reason why women haven't been big winners in business is that they haven't really tried to be. Women have splashed around in the brainwash water, accepting the fiction that they're only number two, until even to them it seems somehow fitting and proper that they should remain in the old familiar employment ghetto. Not quite right—but fitting and proper.

Getting to be the boss is a clear-cut form of winning, and women's conditioned reluctance to take precedence over any man, no matter how incompetent he may be, has been shored up by some exceedingly garbled streetcorner philosophy. Popular sentiment has it that there is something beautiful and lofty about losing and something mean and avaricious in winning.

Well, the nobility that is supposed to crown losing may work fine in nineteenth-century poetry and hillbilly love songs, but it just doesn't play in business. The business world, like all others, is made up of winners and losers. The winners get the tangible rewards—the promotions, the pay, the perks, the privilege of calling the shots that put their plans and wishes into action. The losers get to do the jobs that make all these plans and wishes come off as intended.

Popular sentiment notwithstanding, no matter what anybody says or recites or sings, winning at business or anything else is an exhilarating experience—almost like being in love. Watch a football star exultantly slamming the ball to the ground after crossing into the end zone for a touchdown. Watch an actor or actress taking a curtain call and lighting up like a Christmas tree to find the whole audience up, in a standing ovation. Watch a sweet little old soul in Vegas hitting the jackpot at last and, with squeals of pure joy, catching the quarters in her skirt folds. And watch Mr. Omnipotence himself at the big company bash where he is introduced as the new chief executive officer responding with pride that is hardly concealed by the steely resolve and inflated dignity that his stratospheric new status demands..Do any of these people look miserable and ashamed? You can bet your sweets they don't—because they aren't!

Underdogs are widely romanticized, but they are exactly what the term implies—under dogs. And they are not even recognized as that until they suddenly start to win. Only when it becomes apparent that they have a chance to overtake the leader does the world begin cheering them on and casting about for a place on the bandwagon. The cheering stops if the astonishing winning streak bogs down, and the underdogs slink quietly back to the doghouse, hoping a few diehards will still be yelling, "Wait till next year." Only comedians can make capital of losing.

Business is always fun when you win. It can be less than delightful when you lose and usually is. You not only miss out on the goodies but may also find yourself subject to the will and whim of some people you don't like or admire at all.

Being a Southerner, I grew up in a "defeated nation." I learned all about the inconveniences and disadvantages of losing at my grandfather's knee, and when *Gone with the Wind* came to town, I cheered Miss Scarlett as she shook the turnips at God and swore never to be hungry again. I had never been hungry for food, but I had developed hungers for other things that are hardly compatible with lost battles and lost causes. So okay. As the Southern version of the Civil War goes, "We weren't whipped! We were starved!" Whatever the reason, the result was the same. The simple fact is we lost. And I wanted that to be the last losing side I was ever on. It wasn't, of course. Heaven knows, I've lost some real heartbreakers all along the way. But I could dream, couldn't I? And in any defeated country, dreaming is the classic sustainer.

I expect to be tarred and feathered next Mother's Day for saying this, but the accusing finger points quickly toward Mom as principal molder of the sex roles that are socially acceptable. Women are the carriers of our prevailing sexual attitudes, just as they are the carriers of certain other afflictions—for example, the hemophilia which was spread through Europe's royal families by Queen Victoria, and malaria, passed along to human sufferers of both sexes by the female anopheles mosquito. Intentionally or not, mothers have been transmitting the notion to boys *and* girls that females are born to bear and rear a man's children, keep his cave clean, keep his sox matched and provide all his other little creature comforts from creative meals to creative sex. It's an honorable occupation for women who do it well and enjoy the job (as many millions do), but the cold, cruel fact is that there are millions more who do not enjoy the job and are no damned good at it either.

There are, of course, some enormously gifted women who are well organized enough to combine a career with homemaking. It wears me out and turns me a terrible shade of green just to think about them. Then there are the women, increasing in number, who have simply swapped jobs with their husbands, working the role reversal full time rather than part time. In some instances, this has turned out to be a happy arrangement; in others, one of the partners has become "touchy" or resentful about it. In any event, adjustments have had to be made to accommodate the new economic needs and social attitudes.

Everybody with half the normal number of brain cells understands that the division of labor agreed upon two centuries ago, when the men and women of America were hacking their way out of the wilderness, needs updating to meet the needs of space-age technology. Still, the attitudes toward women in business (everybody's attitudes, including our very own) remain rooted in the 18th-century notion that men must be the "great achievers" while women cheer them on by providing aid and comfort in various picayune ways. Business has translated this into small jobs for women with, of course, small status and small paychecks. It is, and always has been, the function of management to get as much out of people as it can while giving as little as it can get away with. That philosophy is universally applauded as "good management." And since management has been mostly male, what the women have got is not much. The truth is that women have failed to go after much and must, therefore, assume their share of the responsibility for their status, or lack of it, today.

Most women just don't see themselves as bosses and can't possibly conceive of earning as much as $50,000 a year, and more. Their ambitions are likely to stop in the $10,000 to $15,000 range ("good pay for a woman"), or the bold ones may have dreams running as high as $20,000 to $30,000—but seldom higher. How come?

First off, second sexism is a cultural cliché so totally

entrenched that a great many women see no point in knocking themselves out in a struggle so apt to end in frustration and disappointment. Although they may be loaded with intellect, talent and training, they have been preconditioned to the idea that all that intellect, talent and training are somehow substandard because they have been squandered on a substandard person—a "second," flawed merchandise, "a man with a hole in the middle."

Other women hang back in the bulrushes, hesitating to jeopardize the tenuous gains they've made by striking out for larger ones. These are, mainly, women who've been around for a while and are pleased to have made it into middle management or progressed to another spot conferring minor status and steady income—"good income for a woman."

Still others apply the brakes out of some vague feeling that big success in business is a blow to femininity and might diminish their appeal to men, inflict embarrassment on a husband or lover or maybe even cause loss of face with society at large. Recently I heard one of the most brilliant women in the advertising business say on network television that in her husband's lifetime she would never permit her income to become larger than his; as a result, she had declined salary increases offered by her company. "Jack wouldn't have minded," she said. "He was very proud of my career and absolutely elated with the success I achieved. But—I don't know, I guess I would have felt funny about making more money than he did. Because of what people might say. Friends, relatives, you know."

Finally, there are the women who sincerely feel that it is more blessed to have a man with a juicy job than to have any kind of job of their own. These are the women who would rather be married than be president. They are the women who work only as a last resort and then as a stopgap measure. They sincerely prefer the chal-

47

lenges of homemaking to the challenge of business—at least for a while. But disillusionment can set in at home or office and bring about a switch in roles.

Still, the move from office to home has been more widespread than the home-to-office switch and has been an important factor in the attitudes of the corporate community toward women in business. Recent trends to the contrary, most managements still operate on the principle that female employees are temporary—sure to leave for marriage, childbirth, pastures that are greener for man-hunting or when the need to supplement family income has passed. A close examination of employment records would undoubtedly show that there is also an enormous turnover among men in today's mad scramble for fast advancement. Yet there appears to be a lingering suspicion that male employees are "a safer investment," that the company has a better chance to keep them or that at least they are being trained to make a contribution somewhere else in the field.

You Can't Win 'em All, But Try

It becomes clear, then, that if you have a real career ambition, the first order of business is to convince management that you *mean business*—that you're not just playing around or marking time until you can flee to the sanctuary and security of home. This is still difficult for women to do, even the more self-assertive ones. Apparently our cultural attitudes have not changed as much as we have been led to believe. And that may be due largely to the fact that winning, when a woman does it, is often condemned as unfortunate, unfeminine and unforgivable—a misdemeanor, if not a felony, against nature. It's been eons since I believed that one.

My second-grade teacher was a disciple of De Sade

whose idea of a dandy Friday afternoon was to pit the boys against the girls in a competition involving the multiplication tables. They don't honk around in Mississippi about the finer things in life, like six times eight, and Miss Jennie Williams got her jollies teaching us the esoterica of multiplication by organizing "The Great Friday Number Races."

Two walls of the classroom were covered with huge blackboards and on each Miss Jennie arranged the numbers, two through nine, out of sequence, like so:

$$7 \quad 4 \quad 8 \quad 5 \quad 2 \quad 9 \quad 3 \quad 6$$

An uneasy little boy and a miserable little girl were commanded to stand at each board with chalk poised in midair until Miss Jennie shouted out the magic number to be multiplied: "Eight!" Wildly the two terrified antagonists chalked a sum under each number on the board before us and if we did it right, it came out this way:

7	4	8	5	2	9	3	6
56	32	64	40	16	72	24	48

The child who finished first, without error, remained at the blackboard to take on the next challenger of the opposite sex until finally there was one undefeated boy-child and one undefeated girl-child at each board. On those black Fridays the final round usually found me matched against Clifton Hinson, the only kid in the class who could beat my brains out at the multiplication tables —which he did at least half the time. The grand prize was a pencil, an Eberhard-Faber Ebony with a satin lead— to this day, the writing instrument that appeals to me almost erotically, more than any other. When I won it, my joy was unconfined; I felt like Babe Ruth blasting out a grand-slam homer or Catfish Hunter on the final pitch of a no-hitter. And on the days when I lost, it was a catastrophe, the end of the world. To me, that Eberhard-Faber Ebony pencil became the prize beyond any price. And it didn't even have an eraser.

Curse you, Jennie Williams—you and your Friday afternoon number races! They filled me with a yen to win so deep that I've never been able to understand (or even stand) anybody who doesn't share the passion. This, of course, makes losing doubly tough for me, and as they say, "you can't win 'em all." But the only thing that depresses me more than losing is the thought of people not even trying or giving up at the first setback.

In 1976 *Good Housekeeping* magazine introduced a program called "Women in Passage," which, according to Editor-in-chief John Mack Carter, seeks to determine how a cross section of American women feels about the major issues that affect their lives as women and to provide a platform for the presentation of their mainstream views. At the first conference held by participants in the program, Dr. Estelle Ramey, an executive board member of Georgetown University, cited statistics indicating that women are more easily discouraged in their career pursuits and quicker to abandon lofty ambitions than men. Dr. Ramey pointed out that fewer than 2 percent of the women who flunk out of medical school tackle the course again, while 25 percent of the men who fail try again and again and again until they make it. She said this at the conference:

> The young men who have determined to be doctors will even go out of the country to get medical degrees when they have exhausted possibilities in the U.S.A. But over 98% of the young women won't even make a second effort here. It's as if they concentrated all their physical and emotional energies on one big attempt, and when that doesn't work out

the first time around, their sense of rejection is so
deep they abandon the big ambition.

You and Your Big Kakorrhaphiophobia

Fear of failure is a strong motivating factor in business, often as strong as the lure of the prizes that come
in the brightly tinseled package labeled success. When I
was writing advertising for the Hilton Hotels at McCann-
Erickson, Russ Johnston, who was management service
director for this account, activated a research project
concerning the emotional responses of men at work on
projects away from home base. The idea was to collect
information that would help hotels provide more useful
services for businessmen. The research showed that fear
of failure was the dominant emotion of these stalwarts
conducting business away from the security of home and
office, far removed from the assistance provided by wives
and secretaries.

I telephoned Kay Dodge, the McCann-Erickson li-
brarian. Cursed with total recall, Kay can give you an
instant answer to the unlikeliest questions in Christendom
or find one for you in five minutes.

"What's the psychiatric term for fear of failure,
Kay?" I asked. "There must be a phobia in there somewhere."

"Good grief!" she grumped. "The things you crazy
people ask for. I'll call you back."

Five minutes later she did. "Hi. This is Kay Dodge.
The word is kakorrhaphiophobia. And I hope you get it
—bad enough to go home and leave me alone!"

Russ and I had a grand time doing a campaign on
the fear-of-failure theme. The headline was: YOU AND
YOUR BIG KAKORRHAPHIOPHOBIA. The campaign never
ran because in those innocent days of the mid-1960s

somebody in the Hilton organization decided the headline was "suggestive."

Although Russ was altogether macho—a former fighter pilot and trick motorcycle rider—he was relatively untinged by male chauvinism and was concerned about the lack of attention that hotels give to women who travel. I complained bitterly about the short shrift we got (and still get) from hotels and airlines and was delighted when he finally talked our client into designing some rooms that would meet the particular needs of women. The rooms we visualized would be a total departure from the Hotel Contemporary decor that usually greets the weary female traveler. There would be none of the dark colors chosen mainly because they don't show dirt. Instead, the rooms would "dance with light, bright flower tones— sunny yellows, giddy pinks, springy greens." They would also provide a sewing kit, a makeup mirror and "special grace notes" such as boudoir lamps, fluffy throw rugs and a $15 item that became the number one choice of the petty larcenists who delight in liberating objects of one kind and another from hotel rooms—a petite arrangement of ceramic flowers in a small ceramic pot.

The Hilton management balked at the idea when Russ first presented it. What would happen when these "ladies' rooms" (they were, of course, called Lady Hilton Rooms) were not rented to women and the accommodations were needed for men? Wouldn't men refuse to accept a room with so much "feminine atmosphere"?

Canny Russ pointed out that most adult men sleep in women's bedrooms anyway and would feel more at home there than in the neuter surroundings of a standard hotel room. He was right. A number of Lady Hilton Rooms were created in the chain's major hotels, and they proved to be so popular with men that many a man traveling alone requested one. Those Lady Hilton Rooms —now gone—would probably be savaged by the more militant feminists among us today. But they were pure luxury for weary businesswomen—and men.

Fear of success is, perhaps, even more handicapping to women in business than fear of failure. Our well-documented fear of extraordinary personal achievement is still very real because the social and sexual pressures that sent the female competitive drive underground are still around. Accustomed as we are to pleasing men, currying favor with men, looking to men for strength, leadership, authority, even domination, it seems all wrong or, at least, mixed up to be suddenly competing with them for the same jobs, the same salaries, the same rank and recognition. So it follows that a big reason why women haven't won very much in business is that they haven't really wanted to. Even the ones who have made the loudest noises and most energetic motions about it have been strangely torn. And half of winning at any-thing is wanting to.

None of this is meant to imply that only bosses are winners or that every woman should be a boss. Success and satisfaction are earned when a job—any job—is well done. One of the commonest complaints in business is "too many chiefs and not enough Indians." It is the Indians, after all, who support the whole super-structure. But must all of them be women? And must all the chiefs be men?

If you want to catch the big brass ring in business, the first sexual prejudice to get around is your own. Your status needn't be determined by your gender. Here are some things to think about:

1. *Ask yourself if you actually want to be a Boss Lady.* If you don't like the idea of deciding what to do, telling other people how to do it and being responsible for the way they do it, this role is not for you. Do your winning as a terrific Indian.

2. *If you decide that a Boss Lady role is your dish, let it be known.* This is not to suggest that you go charging into the big boardroom on a fire-breathing stallion and challenge the man at the head of the table for his job—or even demand that he crown you with an immediate vice-presidency. Just let it be understood from the first that you expect to go up in the company and intend to turn in a performance that will make management glad to welcome you onto the first team. Make it the first order of business to prove that you mean business about your career.

3. *Be prepared to make personal sacrifices and a lot of them, especially in terms of time and your private life.* The men at the top certainly do. The sacrifices are often harder for women—especially those who have the responsibility of running a home and looking after children. As has been pointed out so many times before, success is more difficult for women to achieve because they do not have wives. Responsibilities at home, in fact, are often cited by management as a disqualifying factor for the promotion of women. If you have a husband who will share these responsibilities or even stay home and take on all of them, congratulations!

4. *Do not ask for or expect special consideration on grounds of gender.* Male or female, anybody who achieves big success in business makes big concessions, and if you accept equal opportunity, you must turn in equal performance, regardless of any extraordinary difficulties involved.

Tough? Yes. Unfair? Probably. But as the saying goes, "Business is business."

4

Packaging Yourself

It's what's inside that counts, but it's what's outside that shows. If your facade doesn't blend with the landscape where you've landed, your genius may not get the chance it deserves to come shining through.

It may seem ridiculous that in an era marked by independence of thought and action, grown women should look for guidelines about putting themselves together, but letters to the editors of virtually every magazine and newspaper indicate that they do. Now that "anything goes," the problem in business is knottier than ever because as far as most management teams are concerned, anything goes *only* as long as it goes their way.

All business organizations, big and little, have an established management style, and clothes usually provide the clue. Men can tell at a glance what the prevailing style is: shirt sleeves, Brooks Brothers-type suits, sports jackets, green suits (à la J. C. Penney), the silk threads of the Seventh Avenue tycoons, the blacks and pinstripes of the Mafia, Gucci loafers, Gucci loafers with the buckles cut off and (God forbid!) polyester "leisure suits."

Since there aren't enough female executives in most companies to provide a pattern, there's nothing to do but play it safe. Until you learn the territory, dress like a candidate's wife—to offend no one! Take a cue from the female newscasters and soap opera stars on television. From Barbara Walters to the-woman-he-loves this week on *As the World Turns,* all of them wear simple contemporary clothes, simple, easygoing hairstyles and simple, noncommittal facial expressions. You may hate it, but that's the way the game is played. Once you've learned your way around corporate attitudes, you can put a little more variety in your life—or a little less, depending on the responses "up there."

If this sounds reactionary, that's only because so many of the top shot callers are. Any deviation from the norm makes them nervous—and the norm is whatever they've decided it is. What most of them have decided about the appearance of women at the office is (you've got it!) that they should dress like a candidate's wife—to offend no one.

Naturally you may assert your independence if you feel suffocated by the prevailing climate, but be prepared to pay the price. The price may be loss of a promotion you've worked your heart out to get, a salary increase you're expecting and need like crazy or a particular program you're trying to get under way. But you'll have the satisfaction of having struck a blow for fashion freedom. I hope it's worth it.

I have a client who wouldn't buy a gold brick from me for fifteen cents if I had on a pants suit when I made the offer. He doesn't like women in pants, body-wrap stoles, clunky shoes, "funny hats" or avant-garde styles of any kind. So unless I feel like throwing away two weeks of hard labor, when I present a campaign to him I wear a nice quiet dress and do my best to look like the friendly neighbor in *As the World Turns*. I express myself through my choice of clothes when I'm not working.

Any woman incensed by these paragraphs may find comfort in the fact that men also have job problems with clothes. At IBM, for instance, as recently as the summer of 1977 management turned down a petition to waive the requirement that men wear regular suits, dress shirts and ties to work. The petition had pointed out that women at IBM are allowed to wear comfortable casual clothes (short sleeves, low necks, lightweight fabrics) in the summer and requested that men therefore be permitted to come to work in sports shirts without suit coats and ties. Management's reply was a polite but firm "No!" IBM wanted clothes at the office to mirror the dignity of the company and the serious nature of its commitment to machines and systems. And since it was the men who made the image, it was these men's clothes that made the difference. The thermostat was kept at the levels suggested by President Carter, and any man who felt too warm was permitted to remove his jacket and hang it in his office, ready to be put back on if he stepped outside. But the jacket as part of office attire remained mandatory!

The wider clothing choice that women generally enjoy nowadays is a blessing with a built-in curse. Narrowing the range down to a personal style is one of life's more harrowing delights—more harrowing than delightful when the decisions involve the office. Clothes that are too trendy, too sexy or too expensive can get you labeled as frivolous or unrealistic—not the sort of woman to entrust with important responsibilities. On the other hand, clothes that are out-of-date, sexless or not expensive enough to reflect the company's status can get you kissed off as insignificant. I didn't think this up and can't say that I agree with it, but I do think it's as petty to fly in the face of these clothing decrees as it is to invoke them.

Any discussion of women's apparel usually wanders into the question of whether women dress to please men or to impress other women. The men taking part in the conversation can be counted on to insist that their own male pleasure is the motivation. The women usually smile and say something like "Not *me,* of course—*I* dress to please myself. But most of the girls I know dress to make some other woman want to kill herself!"

The braless fad has created an uproar at the office among men who enjoy it, women who don't have the mammary endowment for it and people of both sexes who profess to be shocked by it. In the advertising business, where we struggle to be contemporary without chancing a turnoff of customers who might buy what we're selling, it has presented an agonizing problem. Irvin Feld, a client of mine who owns forty-two stores in West Virginia, Maryland and Pennsylvania, was caught in the wringer last spring when a new artist on his advertising staff illustrated a T-shirt on a bra-free figure with nipples clearly indicated. After the ad appeared in newspapers throughout the Feld territory, the stores received a small avalanche of mail, mostly anonymous, declaring in one way or another that bralessness is next to godlessness. The advertising manager was in a state of apprehension over the hate mail until he received the following memo from Feld: "Mick—Reluctantly, I have today instructed that artist to round them off. I. F."

If you're the Boss Lady in your corner of the world, odds are that you've reached an age when it's more merciful to yourself to conceal rather than to reveal details of your physiognomy. (Toward the end of her career the fabled stripper Gypsy Rose Lee used to say, "I've got everything I ever had—it's all just lower now.") However, even if you're a bright young thing with the kind of equipment that the braless look was created for, you'll have a better chance to get your plans and wishes put into action when you "round them off." It's difficult for a woman executive to get herself taken seriously in any costume, and it's *damned* difficult to be authoritative with your bra off.

If Clothes Make the Man, What Can a Woman Expect?

A serious career woman dresses to please the people who can increase her salary and get her promoted. Even if you're just starting out, it's a good idea to dress like a junior executive—in clothes that are young-looking but not freaky. If you're an executive already, try to look as if you belong on the next rung up. Wear the best clothes you can afford, but remember that dressing too well can give somebody in management the notion that you're making too much money—or that you're bad for morale because other people at your level may think you're being paid more than they are. In other words, leave your mink coat and real jewelry at home, to be broken out on weekends and after five. If your boss is a woman, don't, *don't* under any circumstances ever outdress her—unless she's the sort who can (and does get) away with looking as if she just hopped out of a boxcar.

Some women can, indeed, make capital of a really unfortunate appearance. These are the ones with "no redeemable features" of face or figure. During the early 1970s one of the best fashion promoters in New York— call her Adele Sommers—worked under the handicap of a 250-pound Humpty-Dumpty frame, an acned complexion and a myopic stare behind quarter-inch-thick glasses. The important fashion editors constantly tapped her for special assignments and would often send her to major department stores across the country to create special fashion promotions tied in with their magazines. When Adele would get off the plane and introduce herself, the store executives who had rushed to the airport to greet the arbiter of international chic would almost go into cardiac arrest. Recovering their composure, they usually were struck with the wisdom that if *Vogue* magazine gave an assignment to a woman who looked like *that,* she must be the smartest cookie in the whole firmament. She just about was.

I knew another woman who was not able to make capital of an unfortunate appearance as Adele did. She was a key executive for a large cosmetics manufacturer— an unlikely match if there ever was one. It was unkindly suggested that she should get a guitar and take up folk singing because she was a hirsute type who regularly sprouted a beard. Being too preoccupied with her work to bother with a little thing like that, she spurned electrolysis, depilatories and tweezers to concentrate on creating products that made other women look or feel beautiful. She was too good at her work not to be made an officer of the company—which she was—but too unattractive to attain rank commensurate with her intellect and talent.

Every woman at work is subjected to microscopic male scrutiny and verbal dissection. Men with mammoth potbellies, flabby jowls and inflated cabooses feel free to comment adversely, and out loud, on a passing female figure that, with a little exercise and dieting, could easily show up in a centerfold. This is disconcerting, embarrassing and infuriating, but you should try to ignore it.

One woman I know could not. She had gained a few pounds and was miserable enough about it already when she heard one of the water-cooler commentators remark to his fellow men that it was "too bad—she used to be a perfect 36." That was too much for Kathy. Seething, she stopped, then walked back to face him squarely and said, "Yes, it is too bad. You used to have passable manners. But you're still a thirty-six—in the hatband!" The other men in the group, including the one who was her boss, guffawed. However, her boss felt constrained later in the day to give her a peppy little talk about the importance of "rolling with the punches, laughing things off, not taking casual hallway conversation too seriously." Apparently nobody had the same peppy little talk with her body critic. He never spoke to her again. Six months later, when she was transferred to his section, she knew the cookie wasn't crumbling her way and decided to take a job with another company.

When you package yourself for a career as a Boss

Lady, it's a good idea not to stray too far from the original. If you do, you'll not only be uncomfortable with the stranger under and over your skin, you'll also come off as a crashing phony to the people who are required to catch your act.

There is a strong tendency among successful women in New York to accent their speech in a particular way that inspires a great deal of merry ridicule. Whether they were born and reared in Milwaukee, Houston, Seattle, Dallas, Chicago, Atlanta or the Bronx, whether they were schooled at one of the famed "Seven Sisters" colleges or at Corn State U, the day they acquire executive rank they acquire with it an accent that would baffle Henry Higgins. Since it appears to dominate the fashion industry and its press, the language has become known as Fashionese—pronounced, as its adherents have it, FAH-shon-ese. It is an odd amalgam of mispronounced French and British-accented English. The short-*a* sounds are broadened into *uhs,* and so are the *er* sounds, as in uni-VUH-sity. Try not to do this. The broad-*a* sound seldom works outside the British Empire, and Americans are notoriously inept at pronouncing French. My Texas-born friend Delight Wallace has lived in Paris for fifteen years and still can't go home in a taxi because she can't pronounce the name of the street she lives on—in spite of the fact that her husband is a linguist. "It's got four *R*s in it," she says, "and unless you get your French *R*s right before you're four years old, they never sound right to a Paris cab driver."

Sometimes a trip to a faraway place can trigger the use of Fashionese. I once worked with a copywriter who went to London as Peggy Glass and returned five days later as lo! Piggy Glahss. It was six months before she reverted to her normal New Jersey speech patterns, to the consummate relief of one and all.

Having been born and reared in Mississippi, I have

the South in my mouth. A Southern accent is perhaps the most persistent speech taint of all—and the most controversial. Some people associate it with antebellum mansions, magnolias in the moonlight and a kind of misty gentility; others identify it with sharecropper shacks, lynch mobs and the stereotypical stupidity portrayed in the movies and on television. Both schools can find something to love or loathe in my own mixed-up speech.

Wally Miller loathed it. One of my first jobs in New York exposed me to the petty tyranny of one Wallace Walton Miller, who was not actually my boss but might as well have been. Because he controlled a major account at the advertising agency where I worked, he was a man to be reckoned with by everyone on the premises. Life with Wally was no barbecue at Twelve Oaks. He was unfailingly nasty even to the few people he liked, and he dearly loved me not. To him, my accent was not mansions and magnolias but pure potlikker. Every time I opened my mouth in his presence he said something "witty" about collard greens and corn pone, cold grits and pork grease or "dem happy darkies swingin' by the neck from the cottonwood trees."

Wally's sarcasm eventually reached me so deeply that I determined to *do* something about my down-yonder accent and went to a "speech therapist" named Oliver. It developed that Oliver not only gave speech lessons but taught singing, dancing, modeling and meditation, conducted exercise classes and gave scalp treatments. Oliver also cast horoscopes, cut hair, mixed potions for skin problems, communicated with the dead as a medium and was a messenger for CBS. He also had an alcoholic brother who roused himself from an Army cot periodically to pass among the student body serving jelly glasses full of cheap port. Adding to the din was the resident cat, a mangy, one-eyed monster that seemed to be perpetually in heat. An evening at Oliver's was better entertainment than anything on Broadway—or worst than anything Off Broadway, depending on one's tolerance at the moment.

I spent two hours a week at Oliver's studio, fascinated with the panorama and trying to free myself of the Southern accent by reading aloud with a cork between my teeth. After a couple of months I no longer talked like a Dixie dropout; I talked like a woman with a cork between her teeth. I decided then that there are worse things in the world than a regional accent and Wally Miller. Instead of going to Oliver's, I started going to St. Patrick's Cathedral and sitting there until I felt better about what God had given me. It didn't help my speech, but it did help my relationship with my illustrious tormentor. It isn't possible to think about Wally Miller in St. Patrick's Cathedral. Or anybody else you can't stand.

I flew happily back into my natural speech patterns, and while I'm sure there have been times when they didn't serve me well, there have been so many times when they did that I have made peace with my Southern accent and never feel chagrined to have the South in my mouth anymore. People who don't trust "those Madison Avenue slickies" seem to feel reassured when they hear it. It has the ring of reality, and in a business that is often damned as insincere, phony and worse, that can be a valuable asset.

The same thing goes for an accent that is Midwestern, Downeastern, Jewish, Italian, Brooklynesey, Bronxy or whatever. Sooner or later you're going to get excited and lapse into it anyhow, so you might as well relax and let it give you a little memorable color. Besides, it can compensate you for having to dress according to the prevailing management standards. If your clothes clash with the accepted company standard, you can appear to be flouting "policy," but nobody can accuse you of being indifferent to management's wishes if you talk like a native of wherever you come from.

Why Don't We Fix Up This Place? Give It Some Class, Make It *Say* Something!

Office decor is part of an executive's packaging, and this again gives women problems that men don't have. In some companies it's no problem for anybody because the master plan adopted by the corporation leaves nothing to the discretion of an office occupant. At CBS, for instance, when the network headquarters moved into the dark, austere building known affectionately as Black Rock, word came down from Messrs. Paley and Stanton that absolutely nothing could be added or taken away from a desk, wall, windowsill or any other inch of space on the premises. That went for all personnel and all personal property—from ashtrays and pencils to philodendron plants and family pictures. The ensuing anguished baying could be heard all over town, and finally, the employees prevailed. The rules were relaxed to allow a reasonable amount of self-expression. Now desks, walls and windowsills are a cheery litter of posters, ferns, cartoons, balloons and birthday cakes. It's always somebody's birthday at CBS, and somebody has always brought in a decorated cake.

Most companies, however, allow executives to decorate their offices any way they please, and the Boss Lady is likely to hesitate before indulging herself in the pleasure. Should her office look the same as those occupied by the men, or would this make her appear "too butch"? Should she opt for soft, colorful decor, or would this create an impression that she's unbusinesslike or even frivolous? Should she do something terribly chic, or would this cause someone to comment that the new Boss Lady seems to be a bit of a snot?

One of the recent books on how to succeed in business, Michael Korda's *Power!*, described a female executive who appropriated blue as "her" color. She wore blue —and nothing else but. She filled her office with the same shade, floor to ceiling and wall to wall, had the filing cabinets in her department painted "her" shade of blue and extended her territory by invading other areas with similarly colored cabinets, spreading them along the corridors like the blue plague. According to the author, the blue encroachment worked, but my experience tells me that this kind of space appropriation would work only in the pages of a book. I can hear the real-life reaction now: "Who the hell put these stupid blue files here? Get 'em back where they came from before I have them thrown in the goddamn trash!" People guard their turf at the office the way wild animals guard theirs in darkest Africa, and it's my guess that the blue lady with the blue files would have her color scheme interrupted by sudden gushes of red.

The first headlong flights from standard office decor were made by the advertising agencies when the "creative" people decided that their creativity should be expressed by their surroundings. Taking a cue from Howard Gossage, who headquartered his agency in a San Francisco firehouse, they began setting up shop in houseboats, lofts, abandoned churches and other unlikely places, furnished with barber chairs, jukeboxes, slot machines, gutted grand pianos painted purple and pink, wooden Indians, merry-go-round horses and assorted other bits of creative junk. These were the treasures of the 1960s and early 1970s when what I call the "attic and ashcan" culture was in full flower.

Before that the first middle-management originality I saw in agency decorating was brought about by a fashion director, Jill Simmons, who felt a responsibility to *do something different*. Jill ripped down her office-beige draperies and replaced them with white tier curtains adorned with red ball fringe. On the windowsill was a lineup of living red geraniums, and outside her door was a lineup of unbelieving men, waiting to see if it was true about Jill Simmons' office. The humor level sunk as low as red balls and plant lice, but Jill stuck to her geraniums and fringed curtains.

The most fantastic office I ever saw was decorated for her own use by "Estelle Drummond," who sold her company to a conglomerate—and not only stayed on as chairman of the board but managed to see to it that her title did not become an empty honor. Even a retired general of the Army, ceremoniously installed as company president, was carried out on his shield, broken and bleeding, after attempting to depose her. Estelle was like a woman who at a time of stress sells her baby, only to want it back when the stress has passed. When anyone attempted to care for the baby, an obstreperous infant in need of diapering, Estelle reacted with the rage of a mama bear. She became known as Old Stepmother, and being more stepmotherish than old, she was anything but ineffective.

Decorating was one of the outlets for Estelle's festering rage, and she exercised it with more flair than conformity to the established style of the conglomerate. The result could be described only as fantastic, in the most literal sense. In her own office, windows and walls were draped with a heavy tapestry fabric woven in a design described by an incredulous male associate as Little Italy Funeral Parlor. Exquisite antiques of near-museum quality crammed the room, creating the impression that entry should be barred by a velvet rope. Only the brave dared cross the threshold of this elegant shrine and place anything as inelegant as the human rear end in one of her priceless chairs.

Somewhere between Jill Simmons' girlish decor and Estelle Drummond's overwhelming splendor, there has to be an office style that is acceptable to both the woman who presides over it and the people who conduct business with her there. First of all, it should be comfortable for her, equipped with whatever she needs to do her job effectively and with the trappings that please her tastes—without risking a turnoff to those who do not share them. It should also be comfortable for other people, with an easy atmosphere that will not make a visitor feel self-conscious or out of place. I visit a number of executive offices that were obviously designed to impress clients and intimidate job applicants. They usually do just the reverse—that is, impress the job applicants and intimidate clients. And sometimes they may make clients wonder whether "this outfit is making too much money and probably throwing away mine." Showmanship is fine, but too much of it, rather than spell creativity, can look like a substitute for talent.

This is not to say that the office should appear to be the focus of a very necessary economy drive. The idea is to create a setting that suggests a healthy profit, as well as a brisk, businesslike approach.

The most expensive piece of furniture in my own offices is my desk chair, the most comfortable one I could find because I spend long hours in it. It is an unimposing, low-backed swivel, upholstered in a predominantly red geometric print. Bright colors cheer me up, so there are a lot of them around, cooled off by a quiet carpet. When men come in to see me, I usually leave the desk and sit with them at a round table where there is no implied authority. All points in a circle are equal, and I get along better with men in an atmosphere of easy equality. Besides, I don't enjoy feeling barricaded behind a desk when I'm talking with anybody.

You Needn't Kiss Me, but Come On In

An approachable manner is a good personality trait for the Boss Lady. As already observed, the authority figure is seldom welcome whoever it is, and when the embodiment is female, the situation can become more difficult. But it needn't. The best way for a Boss Lady to avoid that is to be friendly, open and easy to get along with. That doesn't mean that she has to go along with the gag by endorsing a plan she doesn't agree with. It means that when she disagrees, she expresses her point of view with diplomacy, mixing in as many yeses as she can with the necessary nos. When men come on shouting and bull-dozing, they are being "forceful"; women who try this approach are unattractively "aggressive."—in a word, bitchy.

There is a quality called presence that is priceless to a woman in business. It is a cool but not cold demeanor—a quiet unflappability that goes along like Ol' Man River.

One of the most successful businesswomen I know is unquestionably the best packaged. She is Dorothy Gregg, the corporate vice-president for communications at Celanese. Dorothy is also a wife, mother and concerned community leader, about whom it is joked that she has been the president of everything except the United States. Approaching fifty, she is a slim, good-looking and "with it" woman. At five feet four inches she could be Mrs. Average America in size, but she "stands tall," "sits tall" and "speaks tall." Her clothes are "conservative chic" (accented by Zuñi Indian jewelry from her native Arizona), and her office is "contemporary comfort." Because she is a Ph.D. economist, the package is smartly topped off with a title—Dr. Dorothy Gregg.

Dorothy grew up on ranches in the Southwest.

"Ranch life," she says, "is active and vigorous. Everyone is a workaholic because you have to be to survive. As a small child I was encouraged to run myself ragged at work and games, to be independent, be a leader, find out what makes things go or grow. I was expected to take risks, great and small, and to learn as much from failures as successes. I was always first to jump from the highest haystack, and if I got hurt, it taught me to make a better jump or use better judgment next time." Looking at her today, you'd never guess that the elegantly put-together package has the rough-and-tumble determination of a ranch hand inside her, but you'd better believe it's there.

The origins of successful women are as varied and different from each other as the backgrounds of successful men, but they all have one thing in common: They learned hard work, independence and leadership at an early age, and whatever else happens, these always are part of the package. Here are some things that I've found to be helpful in the matter of personal packaging:

1. *At any level of business from day one, package yourself as an executive.* And at every level try to look and act as if you belonged at least one step higher. Don't spend beyond your salary range, but do make yourself as presentable as you can.

2. *Don't defy management custom in picayune matters such as dress.* If the prevailing style is conservative, save your avant-garde clothes for weekends and evenings. You don't have to agree with the custom, but it is important to go along with it. Even in the revolting 1960s, when the litter-basket school of fashion prevailed, the big, important corporations did not abandon their standards, and there is scant evidence that they intend to do so now. Managements are notoriously touchy about appearances, and looking out of place could get you out of the place quicker than you can change clothes.

69

3. *When you become a Boss Lady or a bigger Boss Lady, don't give yourself sudden "airs."* Also, don't let the regional bias of an associate push you into another mold. Accented speech is all right as long as it's intelligible and really your own. It can even make what you say more believable—and memorable.

4. *Arrange your office for your own comfort and efficiency, but be sure your visitors are comfortable there, too.* If you feel that the man or woman across the desk from you is annoyed by your authority, why rub it in? Sit someplace where there'll be an easier exchange and you'll have a better chance to carry your point amicably. Of course, if the occasion demands that you invoke your authority, stick to your guns on your side of the desk.

5. *Don't go overboard decorating your office or yourself either.* You want people to pay attention to *you*—don't you?—not where they are or what you're wearing.

6. *Practice an open, approachable manner.* Being remote and aloof does protect you from unwelcome interruptions, but it also seals you off from the day-to-day realities of business. One of the complaints heard about bosses most often is that they don't have the foggiest idea what's going on. It can be difficult for male bosses to find out and impossible for the Boss Lady who is standoffish and unreceptive. An open door and an open ear are always helpful.

5

More Power to You!

"God," Freud wailed, in his most-quoted moment of frustration, "what do women want?" Funny he should ask. One would think he might have picked up the answer from the female parade passing through his chambers in a time and place when it was possible to put women down with a clear conscience, as the good doctor's own question proves.

Well, lie down right here on the couch, Dr. Freud, and I'll tell you what women want.

Women want power.

And that's not "nice." Ask anybody, male or female, in or out of business. Having a taste for power is roundly denounced as an unattractive trait for either sex. Rulers have always been, and still are, prime targets of assassins —fair game for secret knives, guns, poison and bombs, as well as cocktail-party quips, bitchy but entertaining gossip and a relatively new weapon called investigative reporting.

Again, is this any spot for a woman to be in? Men don't think so, but the male bosses seldom mention this as a reason for keeping women out of the hot power spots. They, understandably, do not like to dwell on the vulnerability of their own soft underbellies or their need to be armed and armored. Most of these titans will tell you with ringing sincerity and conviction that the trappings of office don't matter, that the satisfaction of doing the job is more important than any amount of power that comes with the territory.

Forget that. Desire for power is the motivating force

behind most male effort, no matter what the men say. And reprehensible though it may seem, women crave power, too. In the past we have had protection, privilege, prerogative, influence, deference, roses, Godiva chocolates and a lot of other ego-tickling treats, little and big, that have been comforting but definitely not the same as power. Women have been beatified in song and sonnet, glorified at the furriers, jewelers and Cadillac agencies where the sables and minks, diamonds and sapphires, Fleetwoods and Eldorados have identified them as the pampered darlings of men who've got it made. A great many women relish their roles as walking, rolling, flashing ads for the super status of husbands, lovers and other strangers. But a great many others prefer status of their own—in a word, power.

Most of the women of Freud's generation felt constrained to settle for less. But the winds of revolution that have stormed through the ranks of the world's "second-class" people have blown at last into the women's camp, full blast. And the revolt of a whole sex has to be the most affecting rebellion of all.

That Sweet Taste of Honey Is Downright Addictive

Revolutions usually begin with a simple reaching out for equal rights. All that the downtrodden want is equality —at first. But when De Tocqueville's famous "taste of honey" touches the lips of the revolutionaries, the focus swiftly shifts to an open demand for power: power to nail down gains; power to redress wrongs; power to do unto the bastards what the bastards have done unto them!

The drive for black rights, after the first shaky successes, quickly escalated into a rallying cry for Black Power, and the dynamic slogan became inspiration for dozens of imitators, some serious, some comic, some seriocomic. The craze, of course, spread to advertising, where "Pucker Power," coined for a mouthwash, became part of the national hogwash. In Louisiana the long-suffering Cajuns, who ten years ago might have killed you for calling them Coon Asses, swept one of their own into the statehouse as governor on the slogan "Coon Ass Power." The governor's mansion was a long way from the boathouses of his humble and often humiliated antecedents, but Coon Ass Power provided a shortcut for Governor Edwin Edwards.

It is no surprise that women have remained low-"people"-on-the-totem-pole in the universal power surge because gender, simple gender, is as strong and meaningful a characteristic as skin color, age, creed and national origin. This does not mean that I think a dowager living at Beekman Place in Manhattan has more in common with an Indian woman living on a reservation than she has with a male executive on Wall Street. But I do believe that the dowager and the Indian woman are equally ill-equipped to compete with men of their own world.

The tactics employed by militants in the women's movement have not been reassuring. In his history of America since the 1930s, *The Glory and the Dream,* William Manchester observed that "every great moment in history has its sleazy exploiters and souvenir salesmen." This, regrettably, has been the case with the women's revolution, which has often been cynically exploited and peddled for profit like some cute souvenir. The cameras do, of course, follow the freaks, and as soon as the press and television crews have shown up, some self-appointed women's "leaders" have started straining every cell and sinew to attract newspaper space and on-camera time. Such antics made it easy to caricature the whole movement, easy for its opponents to dismiss all women who aspire to personal achievement as a pack of fanatics.

Needless to say, none of the freakism has stirred much sympathy in the hearts of men. It has been welcome news only to the gentlemen of the press, who could hardly wait to headline it in the next editions of their papers and highlight it on the six o'clock news—the latter with numerous merry side comments to their female cohorts on the television programs. Out there on the other side of the front page and the idiot box, even women and men who have been high on the drive for equality of the sexes have read the quotes with rising trepidation, gazed balefully at the movement's big mouths and finally decided, "Whatever *they're* for, *I'm* against."

The movement has been exploited not only by some of its female innovators but by a great many men who may be against the underlying philosophy but are definitely not against making a buck on it. The built-in opportunities are irresistible, and merchandisers have been quick to hop aboard the medicine wagon to market feminist T-shirts, aprons, buttons, bumper stickers, banners, umbrellas, books, movies, plays, television programs, pens and pencils, note pads, wall plaques, lingerie, sleeping garments, bed linens and G-strings. One man has even made a career of standing on Fifth Avenue at Rockefeller Center plugging something he is pleased to call Husband Liberation. He drapes himself with ankle-length sandwich boards which are littered with homemade signs pleading for male dominance among the lawfully wed. New Yorkers don't pay much attention to him, but he evidently sells enough of his "literature" to tourists to stay in business there.

Some defenders of the feminist faith insist that even the outrageous antics of the big mouths have been beneficial to the cause because they have "thrown light" on the problem. But when some of those overwrought creatures go into their act, the dark is light enough. The big mouths have proved embarrassing to serious career women, causing some of them to deny their own ambition with the alacrity of Peter denying Christ. But the basic situation remains unchanged. Women still want power.

It May Be in the Cards, but It's Not in the Books!

Power is a complex and often baffling phenomenon, endlessly fascinating to the haves and to the have-nots. In the past few years bookstores have been flooded with texts about power: what it is, how to use it, how *not* to use it and, most of all, how to get it. Recently the books have begun to focus on woman power, with both male and female authors advising, instructing and lecturing women on the subject—as though it might be chocolate cheese cake based on a tested Betty Crocker recipe.

The books contain pointers that work brilliantly in some instances and bomb resoundingly in others. There are, of course, no foolproof recipes or fail-safe methods for achieving that elusive Nirvana, success! The successful people who are honest about it are quick to admit that one of the larger elements in their rise to glory was plain luck. They got the breaks, and equal employment opportunity notwithstanding, these still go more often and more readily to men.

These books can tell you what the ingredients of power are, but they can't give you much help in putting them together. Business success is a highly individual matter based not only on capability but on that mysterious interaction between people known, for lack of a better term, as chemistry. And of course, there are the breaks.

The power tactics that succeed for men in business almost never work for women. They must be refined, moderated, varied, camouflaged or, more often than not, passed up altogether in favor of an entirely different method of operation. As matters stand now, a woman's approach must be marked by a lot more subtlety and finesse most of the time—especially in the early stages. This does not mean that being female dictates that you should be less than positive in and about your job. It only means that it is easier when you tread softly and remain alert to the reactions around you.

It may annoy you to proceed with the caution of a lovemaking porcupine instead of the force of a charging cheetah, but the reality is this: Men simply won't accept from women the kind of business behavior freely indulged in and cheerfully approved by other men. (Neither will women! The double standard applies for both sexes.)

Nevertheless, women can find useful information in the books written for men who burn to forge ahead in business. You always enjoy any game more when you understand what's going on and can identify the players. Moreover, if you're going to play it yourself, it's essential that you be able to recognize a technique that could block your own goal or score points at your expense. And some of these books on power can help you do just that. They can also teach you how to recognize the leading contenders for power in your organization and how to ally yourself with the potential winners.

If that seems like "conniving," don't brood about it and don't concern yourself with the likelihood that it may be called female cunning. Actually it's exactly what the men do. Watch how quickly they choose up sides! They scent downwind, pick the man in the pack who appears strongest and back him to the hilt—until they sense a shift on the battleground.

Women are well advised to do the same. Only they have to be less obvious about it—and everything else.

"Us Niggers Got to Stick Together!"

In business, power may be defined simply as authority—the authority to make decisions and make them stick. Who is hired and who is fired. Who is promoted and who is banished. Who gets more money, more stock, more say-so and how much. Which programs will be pressed into action when, and which will be scrapped. The men and women who decide these things have the magic: power!

The decision-makers, however, are subject to influence, and the people who exercise influence have power too, *in direct ratio to their ability to exercise it.* In other words, who whispers in the ear of the king or queen also has power.

In business both sexes are more comfortable with female influence than female power because they are more accustomed to it. They are thoroughly familiar with female influence at home and are not unduly surprised or disturbed when it surfaces at the office. But when it becomes clear that a woman in the organization actually wields power of her own, the scene changes. Neither sex is sure how to accept this or whether it's necessary to accept it at all. The knowing ones—the women who have a real understanding of the situation—don't just accept it; they *embrace* it, with a show of grace and enthusiasm. Maybe they don't feel gracious or enthusiastic at all, but at least they go along with the script.

There are always other people of influence to watch for—notably, friends, lovers and relatives of top management. As mentioned elsewhere in these pages, secretaries often have tremendous clout. Additionally there are totally unpredictable power spots, such as the one I encountered when I was writing advertising for one of the world's largest distilleries. He was a twenty-five-year-old black named Buster, a dropout from the third grade who was chauffeur-gardener-valet for the distillery's chief executive. The liquor baron was a highly eccentric man who despised advertising, had no confidence in his own advertising manager but placed great faith in Buster's opinion of the advertising we created for his popular scotches, bourbons and "kitchen whiskey." Since the baron seldom left his estate, the agency group usually journeyed out to his place on Long Island to show him the advertising we had prepared and, we hoped, get his okay. He would spread the magazine layouts and television storyboards across the Oriental rug in his study and bellow for Buster.

"Get the hell out here, Bus, and see what you think of this agency horseshit!"

Buster would shamble into the group, stare ruefully at the material a dozen highly professional advertising people had been working on for six weeks and, without looking up, mutter, "Read me." I would read the copy to him very slowly, taking care to read headlines, too, because I had an agonizing suspicion that Buster couldn't decipher even those large block letters.

After I finished reading, he would continue to stare for eternal minutes more, during which no one dared to speak. Most of the time Buster would finally shake his head in negative bewilderment and announce, "I don' get it!" whereupon the baron would snarl, "Buster don't get it. Do us some more!" We would then trudge back to the agency, where rooms full of high-priced talent struggled to guess what could possibly be said or pictured that Buster *would* get.

On one occasion, when a longtime enemy of his had just died, our beloved client was in a mellow enough mood to explain why he let Buster call the shots. "A lot of people who drink whiskey are just about as smart as

78

Buster," he said, "and have just about as much education. Maybe they went to school longer, but they don't know any more. I figure if Buster gets it, anybody can get it, so I just go with what he says."

The liquor baron may have been a better judge of shrewdness than we realized. For it was Buster who first made me aware of a brutal description that some of the liberationists have since applied to the status of women. Once, when I complained of a headache, Buster disappeared and returned with two aspirin tablets and a glass of ice water. When I thanked him, he said "It's okay, babe. Us niggers got to stick together."

Black man. White woman. Niggers. Funny, I had never felt that being a woman relegated me to epithetsville, and I didn't think of Buster's remark again until the libs declared that women were the gender-niggers. Not a pretty name at all. But neither is "cunt" or "bitch"—two of the favorites that some of the more resentful men have leveled at many an uncunty, unbitchy woman who has asked that her work be taken seriously and that her ambition be respected.

The dirty names are of no consequence. The Boss Lady's reaction to them is. Any woman who aspires to power in business must be prepared for a bit of name-calling. If she genuinely wants to succeed at the work or art she has chosen—whether it's banking or belly dancing, "manning" a manufacturing company or running a rabbit farm, writing, selling, acting, painting, shipbuilding or whatever—she probably has a good, strong sense of self already and a deep commitment to mastering the territory. That in itself is liberating. It not only frees her to grow and succeed but virtually requires her to do the growing that leads to success.

Power is volatile stuff. And handling it or even approaching it calls for skill, if not delicacy. Here are a few guidelines for you:

1. *When you get it, don't flaunt it.* People who aren't used to power often get carried away with the heady glory of it all and act like a whole covey of jaybirds during cherry season. (My grandfather said that the birds get drunk on fermented cherries—the origin of the phrase "crazy as a jaybird.") Overreacting to one's own greatness breeds ridicule, and since power is universally regarded as "male," a woman who flaunts it is inviting the cruelest kind of caricature and mockery.

2. *Don't believe your own press.* The media look for "angles" that can capture the attention of their audiences, and the angle they take on you, good or bad, depends on how it fits into (or breaks away from) a trend of the moment. Just remember that shifting the point of view a few degrees can change the reports about you from praise to damnation—and vice versa.

3. *Teddy Roosevelt said it best: "Speak softly and carry a big stick."* While the memory of this flamboyant Roosevelt does not invoke visions of this philosophy at work, it's still good advice for a man or a woman. And women can accomplish more with soft speech than with any amount of shouting.

6

The Good News and the Bad News: Hiring and Firing

Nothing heats up the spot a Boss Lady is on like the duties of hiring and firing. The thought of either can produce a heady glow, a sense of goddesslike power. Both activities do pack power all right, but wielding it can become one of the real terrors of the territory.

First, there's the dangerous little duty of hiring. Handing out the largess of a juicy job that dozens of supplicants are lined up for may sound like dreamy fun. But the dozens can dwindle when it becomes clear that the boss is mere woman, and the difficulties she experiences in putting together an effective team are often ulcerating.

Making a mistake in your choice of a new team member to bring aboard can be poison to your plans for advancement. It's bad enough to have a weak spot in the ranks, where you had anticipated strong, effective support. But it's even worse to writhe around in the fear that your superiors are up there thinking you're no good at judging people. ("She's a fine executive in some respects but doesn't know how to build a good staff; just can't pick em!")

Picking 'em is always chancy. Male executives run the same risks, but the men have had time enough and experience enough to become clever at concealing their little hiring slips—sometimes by pushing the incompetent for promotion in another area of the company. Executive women are seldom able to get away with this kind of hocus and are reluctant to try it anyway. When they do try it, they're usually so uncomfortable with the situation that it shows. The smarter ones prefer to avoid the problem by moving with all the caution of a high-wire walker when they employ people.

Anne Hyde, who, with Janet Jones, owns the New York executive placement firm called Management Woman, stresses the value of the interview and the importance of giving it undivided attention. "Résumés can give you the facts, but they can't give you much insight into the personality and character of the applicant. Besides, risky though it is, some people do exaggerate their credentials on that piece of paper, and they may also be good enough at playacting to back up the exaggeration unless the interviewer pays close attention to all the little nuances of a personal meeting."

"Virginia Tobin," one of the strongest executives of either sex I've ever met, reinforces Anne Hyde's philosophy. Virginia—who asks to be anonymous because she has a new high-level position with a manufacturer of computer hardware—says she relies heavily on "human chemistry" when she's talking with a prospective staffer. "That first meeting is crucial," she says. "The reaction of two people to each other is vital to the success of a job situation, and I am as aware of my own reactions as those I observe in the other person. Do I really like this individual? Do we think alike, and if we don't, will the differences be destructive or will they create healthy friction? Do we like each other and respect each other's ability? In short, will we get along?

"After that I try to determine how he or she will fit in with the rest of the staff. Will he or she bring new and needed strengths to the department? Be a disruptive addition or a happy, productive one? Is this someone I'll be proud to introduce to my associates inside the company and outside? These are the big questions I keep in mind while I'm examining the credentials of an applicant. All very important—because business does not live by brains alone."

Some companies have dominant personnel directors who insist on doing all the hiring. But you should insist just as firmly on interviewing anyone who is being considered for your department. The reaction that you and the applicant have to each other is vital, and only you can hope to determine accurately how the applicant and his or her qualifications will relate to the department and the other people who work there.

We Love You—but You're Fired!

Firing is an even more difficult task. There may be something very soul-satisfying about the notion of booting out somebody who is upsetting your whole scenario—a real rotter who is incompetent, indifferent or offensive in other ways. But when the chips are down, firing is a chore that can actually be enjoyed only by a certifiable sadist. And you can bet that the same personnel director who wants to do the hiring will cheerfully leave the firing chores up to you.

No doubt you have heard many a successful person talk wittily and fondly of having been fired. "Everybody should be fired at least once!" he or she declares. And typically, the declaration precedes or follows a story loaded with laughs plus a wry twist of good fortune which proves all over again that God is a "very funny guy." The speaker is usually recounting an incident that occurred about ten years ago—ten years being roughly how long it takes for the humor or therapeutic value of the experience to surface. No matter how droll or fortunate the dismissal appears later on, at the time it occurs it can seem like the end of the world.

In short, getting fired is seldom fun, and having to

fire an associate is one of the real agonies of being a boss, unless you are a calloused creature with little or no regard for the feelings of other people. And in that case you probably won't be a Boss Lady long enough to get your jollies from swinging the trusty ax many times. Some bosses avoid the unpleasantness by "selling" good old Charlie to the head of another department in the company; some by convincing personnel that Charlie is much too good for the job he's holding now and should be promoted forthwith—to another area. Here you have one of the answers to that old question about how mediocre men wind up in the high-priced seats with impressive titles, large offices and secretaries who are abler than they are. Firing Charlie, after all, is an admission that the boss (a) can't get him to perform, (by) made a mistake in hiring him or (c) erred in keeping him on if Charlie came with the job.

I refer here to the fireling as male because women are seldom promoted to conceal their shortcomings. Also, as noted elsewhere, they are considered more expendable and less in need of steady income than men. They are, however, often kept around in minor roles because somebody feels sorry for them or responsible for them or just plain reluctant to boot them out.

Firing a man is especially tough for a woman because of the psychology of the situation, given the current state of male-female relations. Even if a man is really champing at the bit to be canned so he can collect severance pay or unemployment insurance while he pursues a special project, getting the news from a woman is a blow to the male ego. And of course, if he wants to keep the job, being fired by a woman can make the experience even more devastating.

The first man I had to fire burst into tears. There was a sudden budget cutback in the company, and one of those orders came down from the upper reaches decreeing that the payroll be cut by 10 percent. I carefully reviewed the roster to determine which duties could be dispensed with, which could be combined in one job instead of being spread across several and, finally, which employees we could struggle along without. Allen Morehead was first choice among the logical ones to go. He had been employed last, was habitually late to work, was often "out sick" and showed little interest, energy or initiative when he was there. I had talked with him about this already, and he had agreed to do better—and to some extent, he had.

On the fateful day I invited Allen into my office, explained about the budget cutback and expressed regret that we could not continue his employment there. I didn't expect him to care because his attitude had been only a shade short of cavalier, but this twenty-eight-year-old man immediately burst into tears, complete with great, body-racking sobs. I was miserable until he sobbed out the news that he was crying not because he minded losing the damned job but because he was being fired by a goddamned woman.

The first woman I had to fire called me the bitch of the year, then asked if she could borrow $10 from me to start a fund for my tombstone. I thought that was a highly creative remark—predictably so, because she was a highly creative person, a fashion illustrator of exceptional expertise. This happened in Mississippi, where there wasn't another illustrator a tenth as talented, and at age twenty-four I was trying to produce advertising of a caliber that could get me to New York.

Helen was what is known as a credit drunk, always deeply in debt because she bought anything that caught her fancy, charged it and never concerned herself with anything so mundane as paying for it. I never understood how a woman with her payment record could get so much credit, but she did get a prodigious amount. Consequently, our department was frequently disrupted by bill collectors, and the personnel director was harassed by Helen's disappointed creditors. We made several attempts to help her solve her problems, but nothing worked. On one occasion the men who owned the store (the brothers Kennington) gave her a sum of money large enough to clear up all her debts and start over. Instead of doing that, she bought an apartment full of new furniture, selling the unpaid-for furniture she had to make room for it.

I suffered a lot with Helen because I knew she had tremendous emotional problems. She said that job pressures caused a tension buildup inside her which could be relaxed only by "buying something." After I fired her, I got a continuing stream of tombstone remarks from her, which switched from my tombstone to hers as she began threatening to commit suicide—usually on the telephone at three or four o'clock in the morning. She finally moved to Cincinnati and is, I guess, still running up bills for furniture there.

Helen was, of course, an extreme case—perhaps the most difficult one of my career—but firing people is always a bad scene. Still, if you're running the show, it's part of the script. If someone in your employ should be fired, don't hesitate. Delay accomplishes nothing except a tension buildup that "buying something" won't help. First, if the person isn't performing as required, talk to him or her about what is needed and expected, where the needs and expectations are not being met and how some changes may be made to meet them. This conversation should give you a good idea of whether the desired improvements in performance can be effected. If you decide on the basis of this talk that it's a lost cause, start trying to line up a replacement, but give the incumbent a fair chance—an agreed-upon length of time for him to shape up. If there is not sufficient improvement, then you should move with strength and conviction, knowing that good old Charlie or Charlene will be happier and more productive in a job that's a better fit.

Some employers, seething with frustration, fire people because they can't think of anything else to do at the moment. Granted, such bosses are wildly neurotic. You don't run into many of them in large corporate structures, but you do meet a lot of them in privately owned companies where they can operate their own firms as they jolly well please. My favorite example was the aging female tycoon whom I call Lori Pushkin, owner of a "high-fashion salon" in Philadelphia. Miss Pushkin was a dictator who could make Fidel Castro look like Camille in the last reel. All she wanted was to be tall and thin, young and beautiful. She was only rich and brilliant. Physically she fell about a foot short of her ideal and burdened a squat sixty-five-year-old frame with about twenty excess pounds. When she was unhappy—which was any time she passed one of the salon's fifty or so mirrors—the slightest irritant could set off one of her notorious temper tantrums. These were near-nuclear explosions which often culminated in her smashing one of the costly pier mirrors with a jade ashtray, an antique lamp or some other little object. In such rages, she would fire anyone standing nearby—usually Ted Wilburn, who came out of his office expressly to be discharged because she always rehired him at a higher salary. "A paltry increase," he said, "but *some*thing to be thankful for." After he had been there a year, he was making almost as much money as she was.

Her other favorite victim was her forty-year-old nephew, Martin, who was also consistently rehired but at a decrease. Martin wasn't stupid, but he was so terrorized by his aunt that he might as well have been. Once, while he was president of the local businessmen's association, he posed for a newspaper photographer kneeling at a cross of Easter lilies with his hat on. She, of course, smashed a crystal sconce and fired him for that—twice. Once when she saw the photograph on the front page of the *Bulletin,* and again when he explained that he didn't mean to show disrespect; he just didn't want to show a bald head.

Miss Pushkin was the only woman I ever knew who literally tore her hair out. She would dart out of her office, roaring, "Why am I so goddamned ineffective?" tearing whole handfuls of her leonine mane out by the roots. The truth was that she was easily the most effective person on the Eastern seaboard since everybody who knew her was too terrified of her to resist anything she determined to do. No detail was too small to command her meticulous attention. If a carpet had to be tacked down, she wanted to see the tack and wanted to interview the man who was going to hit it with a hammer. Needless to say, he never did it to suit her. And she fired him.

Clearly this was all a game with Miss Pushkin. Everybody except Martin (who never learned that it wasn't serious) enjoyed it enormously. She fired me at least a dozen times before it finally happened on a day when I was too depressed to fall into the spirit of the sport. I loved working at her salon but realized that the progress I had not made in a year would continue. So I packed up and caught the train to New York.

There's No Easy Way

In the twenty years that have followed I have had to fire people for offenses as widely diverse as striking a client physically (which I have occasionally ached to do myself) and stealing out of the petty cash (usually too petty to bother with, so anybody who does bother deserves retribution). Sometimes, in a move dictated by changes in management programs or budgeting, I have had to fire people for no offense at all. Whatever the reason, there is always intense discomfort on both sides of the desk. For my part, I would infinitely prefer scrubbing down the bleachers in Yankee Stadium after a World Series. The best I can offer in the way of advice is the following:

1. *Do it quickly and directly* without a long preamble or any rambling digressions.

2. *Soften the blow as much as possible* with any warm words you can sincerely muster about the individual's capabilities and contributions to the company. He or she must have been doing *something* right. Be friendly. Be nice. Be *human*.

3. *State exactly what the company will do* in the matters of severance pay and assistance in relocating. Be sure this is fully understood, and if there's any doubt, put it in writing.

4. *Make it clear that the action is firm and final.* Do not permit yourself to be drawn into argument or debate, and do not agree to an appeal to another authority. Just say you're sorry, and end the meeting.

5. *Do not prolong the interview* with a philosophical discussion about your own or somebody else's dismissal that turned out to be a godsend. That's the last thing a fireling wants to hear.

Fewer duties put a boss, male or female, in a more uncomfortable spot than dismissing an aging executive with a large salary and small chance of landing another job as lofty and lucrative. A recent article in the *New York Times* pointed out that few executives are ever fired, but thousands each year are "displaced," "surplused" or "squeezed." Regardless of the euphemism applied, the reality is the same. The executive must find a new position.

If you have had to do the guillotining, you can take some of the trauma out of it by providing immediate help.

That help is now available to you for the squeezee in the form of a new kind of executive service which is called decruitment, dehiring or outplacement—all cheer-up euphemisms meant to take the sting out of being fired. Owing to the proliferating acquisitions and mergers, business is booming for the firms engaged in this specialty. They customarily charge 10 to 15 percent of the discharged executive's salary, with a minimum fee typically set at $2500; some of the firms have a maximum fee as well. In any event, costs are paid by the discharging company; the executive pays zip. There may be additional charges (also to the company) for printing and mailing client materials such as résumés and "work samples," plus the cost of any consultant travel. Even so, companies footing the bill are saved thousands of dollars on exiting executives since the outplacement service is cheaper than the severance pay which management may be obligated to give.

If your firm maintains its own outplacement activities, you're in luck and may be able to tell Charlie that your company already has a spot lined up for him elsewhere. But the outplacement consultants aren't much concerned with Charlene's plight. In fact, the *New York Times* states that few women or members of ethnic minorities undergo outplacement, since "both groups are still thinly represented in the executive suite and somewhat less subject to firing for fear of legal action."

However, the Boss Lady can and does still get the old heaveho, and if it happens to you, here are some things to do:

1. *Accept the news gracefully and coolly.* Don't make it any more difficult and unpleasant for the news bearer than it is already. The Greeks used to tear out the tongues of messengers who brought bad tidings, but you have to make a farewell deal with the man or woman

giving them to you. You'll get a better one if you're pleasant. Just don't make the ax-person happy that he or she is armed with an ax.

2. *Ask for assistance in locating a position elsewhere.* Discuss outplacement, through either a consulting firm or the facilities and contacts of the company you're exiting.

3. *Negotiate for more severance pay over a longer period of time.* Whatever you're offered, express warm thanks and suggest more.

4. *Ask if you'll be using the same office and secretary while you job-hunt—matter-of-factly because, of course, you'll need them.* Doing this as if you're sure they'll be provided will make it awkward for your Greek messenger to refuse. Besides, you really will need them. Better to have a crisp secretary answering your phone than a kid with a mouthful of peanut butter sandwich announcing to a prospective employer that Mommy's lunching at Lutèce and usually stays there about three hours.

5. *Try not to take an expensive vacation.* Your body may need it, and your soul may be fairly screaming for a deep ego massage, but stick around. It's important to be on hand for interviews, and no matter how inactive the job scene may appear, something may come up besides your breakfast. Also, you may need that money you blew.

6. *Start looking for a job right away.* Let your friends and all your business contacts know you're available, and don't be embarrassed about it. There's a big job turnover going on all the time, and anybody who understands anything understands this.

7. *Swallow your bias against résumés (if you really dislike them), and prepare a careful one.* So, all right— the stupid things don't mean anything to you and a lot of other people, but to some prospective employers they're

only a little less sacred than a relic of the true cross. Job counselors counsel that the purpose of the résumé is to get you an interview, not the job itself. So don't write your autobiography. Keep it short (never more than one page) and professionally provocative. And please, no pictures, no poetry, nothing coy or cutesy.

8. *Put yourself on a tighter budget*. You don't have to turn in an imitation of the poor little match girl, but you don't need to live like Jackie O. either. Don't hesitate to pick up the check if it's your turn, but save the three-hour lunch at Lutèce to celebrate your new job when you've landed it.

9. *Don't belittle your past employers*. It may entertain a prospective employer group to hear what bitches and bastards their competitors are, but it can also start them wondering what you'll say about them.

10. *When you leave the place where you've been fired, be sure to leave them laughing—or at least smiling*. They may decide somebody made a mistake and invite you back someday at a much higher salary. Also, you could wake up some morning to find that your new company has been bought by the old one. Or you could breeze into the office and discover that the new boss just hired there is the very same Mr. Omnipotence who fired you.

7

Help! (Working for a Woman)

"Men don't like to work for women, and women don't either." Everybody says so, and generally speaking, it *is* so. However, the best boss I ever had was a woman. So was the worst—but more about her later.

The men, I can understand. After spending much of their lives under female domination, reined in by moms, nurses, baby-sitters, schoolteachers, wives and assorted others of the opposite sex, they may not rejoice at the opportunity to do the bidding of yet another woman—this time on the job. Also, people of both sexes usually want to work for the most important executive in the company they can. It's a matter of status. At the same time ambitious employees reason that they have a better chance to rise in the corporate hierarchy if their department is headed by a strong person who's going places. In most companies that person is about twenty times more likely to be a man. Finally, there is the stigma of second sexism that causes men to feel marked down when they go striding in to work and report to a mere woman. They don't like the boys in the back room to know about it, or the girls in the front seat either.

The women who harbor this kind of resentment are not so easily understood. The female reluctance to accept a Boss Lady rather than a boss was first brought home to me by a bright, attractive young woman who applied for a job as my assistant. We hit it off wonderfully. The work was exactly what she was looking for, the salary was right and she had every qualification I had hoped to find. As I was at the brink of hiring her, she suddenly asked, "By the way, shouldn't I meet the man I'll be reporting to?"

I laughed merrily and said, "I'm the guy!" expecting this news to be greeted with riotous applause. Nuh-uh! The gleam in her eye flickered into doubt and disappointment. Haltingly, painfully, she said, "Well-l-l, gee now . . . I don't know. I'm sure you're a perfectly nice person and all that, but I just think I'd like it better if I worked for a man."

Since she was to be my assistant, I didn't see how we could pull that one off, and needless to say, I quickly decided not to get involved in the effort. At any rate, hers is an attitude I've encountered a number of times since then. Women have looked me straight in the baby blues, assured me they had nothing against me personally, but said they'd rather work for a man. On several occasions I have asked them (pleasantly, I hope) what they plan to do when they themselves have become bosses and are confronted with this same kind of resistance on grounds of gender. Always they appear startled at the idea and reply, in one way or another, "Oh! Uh, that's different!"

Oh, but it's not. It is exactly the same. Both men and women almost always express a marked predisposition to work under the supervision of a man. Yet male or female, mixed genders or matched, employee-employer relationships, like all others, depend heavily on individual responses to each other, to human chemistry. When the boss is a woman, the chemistry is a great deal more complex and volatile.

It Takes All Kinds—and I've Had Them!

I have had a succession of bosses of both sexes—some wonderful beyond any telling, some god-awful and some so mediocre they are barely remembered. My best boss was Betty Shaver, who was copy chief at the first advertising agency where I worked in New York. Betty had a lightning-swift mind, a delicious sense of the ridiculous—and terminal cancer. A few longtimers at the agency knew she had been fighting the disease for years, but in the eleven months that I worked for her, nobody but Betty knew she was dying. The other newcomers and I didn't even know she was ill.

Betty chain-smoked with a long cigarette holder held at a rakish tilt, not an affectation but an effort to cut down on the intake of nicotine and tar. Her humor took the sting out of the copy editing she did, and when anybody presented her a piece of prose that was overwrought and overwritten, she simply did her imitation of Wagnerian opera and handed it back to the author. Her performance was so admirable and, at the same time, such an accurate evaluation of the ad that even the touchiest copywriter among us could accept the critique.

She knew everything: all there was to know about the English language, baseball batting averages, bus and subway routes, racehorse bloodlines, the products we advertised, the clients who made them—and how miserable I was made by Wally Miller, who goaded me unmercifully about my Southern accent. She didn't treat us all alike, but she did treat us with equal fairness and a rare insight into individual problems. Since people are as unalike as snowflakes, it seems ridiculous even to think about treating them all exactly alike.

I was young, awed by New York as only a country girl from Mississippi could be, and the other copywriters were pointedly unreceptive to my eager-beaver approach. So I needed all the help I could get. Betty was unfailingly helpful, never actually solving problems for me but giving them just enough attention to open my eyes to possibilities and then to enable me to enjoy the vast satisfaction of solving them myself. And whenever I developed a "glass arm," she handled it with characteristic flair.

A glass arm is the affliction that is all too familiar to everybody who writes anything for a living. It attacks viciously and unexpectedly, always when it is least convenient, making it impossible for you to write—even a letter home or a supper slip. The paper before you gets wider and wider, whiter and whiter, until you might as well be lost in the heart of Antarctica. Every time you grasp a pen or strike a typewriter key your arm breaks off at the shoulder and shatters into millions of nasty little shards that wink maliciously up at you from the table.

Whenever this affliction, also known as writer's block, struck me—and in those days it was often—Betty would send me out to an art gallery, to a movie or just "over to Bonwit Teller to charge clothes," knowing that the glass arm goes away after you've immersed yourself in the problem at hand, then set it aside and relaxed. "Take it easy," she kept saying, "because it *is* easy. After all, it's only advertising." Finally, Betty's physical pain became so intense that bourbon didn't help anymore, and she went home to suffer out of sight. She died much too young but has never gone away. Every time I get a glass arm I hear her saying, "Oh, pooh—why don't you run over to Bonwit's and charge clothes?" And I do.

The worst boss I ever had was a large, imposing woman whose identity I will obscure with the name "Gertrude Ashtabula." Gertrude sat at her desk as though she was sitting on a horse, upright and alert to any movement. Her high-backed chair seemed to disappear, and the hapless (yea, hopeless!) subordinate before her was stricken with the impression that she was poised astride a fire-breathing stallion ready to crush any obstacle under thundering hooves. When she rose, her commanding manner made you think of those old World War II pictures of George Patton standing up in the lead tank. Unlike the killer general, Gertrude smiled a lot, flashing a set of Ultra-Brite teeth that caused one of her more uncharitable minions to nickname her Teeth for Two. Now she is remembered simply as Jaws.

Gertrude held a position of great power at the company and was the only woman who did. This led her to look upon herself as the great mother of us all. Except for a few special favorites (all males), she treated each of us, regardless of age, like naughty or slightly retarded children. When I landed in her department, I was thirty-six years old in my stockinged feet, but she had a genius for making me feel six or eight. The most insignificant encounter with her filled me with the uncomfortable sensation that I was a runny-nosed brat about to disgrace herself still further by puddling on the carpet.

To compound the disaster, Gertrude was an imaginary lint picker. She would buttonhole one of her "kids" in the hallway for a friendly little chat and, flashing those two sets of teeth in a thousand-watt smile, pick away at collar and lapels until the accosted creature felt like one of the world's really spectacular slobs—even though we had all checked each other to make certain that everybody's clothes were totally lint-free, dandruff-free and dust-free. I once had a mohair suit which she reacted to like a madly maternal monkey, working over the fuzzy fabric surface until the lapels were picked clean. After two months I had to send the suit to the Salvation Army.

While we could laugh at things like the lint picking, some of the other Ashtabula tactics weren't funny at all and are among the reasons men cite for denying positions of authority to women. Gertrude clearly enjoyed her "only woman who" status and was quick to obstruct the progress of any other woman who showed promise. Salary increases and promotions automatically went to one of her "boys"—that is, men who had so thoroughly convinced her of their doglike devotion that their level of incompetence didn't matter. The other men were treated like the standby cast of an *Our Gang* comedy. She was coy with her superiors and imperious with everyone she outranked, underlining her authority with weekly staff meetings which had no discernible function beyond giving her an opportunity to preside. Since all she presided over was coffee and a tray of Danish, these meetings became known as Gertrude's Tuesdays. I was banished from her department twice before she finally succeeded in getting me sacked by the company, and although I didn't really want to be tossed out, when the inevitable happened I was almost relieved. It's no fun to feel like an eight-year-old slob when you're neither eight nor slobbish but an accomplished professional who can brush her own lapels, blow her own nose and run her own department with dazzling productivity.

Let There Be More Betty Shavers—and a Pox on the Ashtabulas!

If more Boss Ladies had been like Betty Shaver and fewer like Gertrude Ashtabula, maybe it wouldn't be so difficult for those of us who have followed to hire the kind of help we need. Often we're reduced to struggling along with the kind of staff we'd be better off without:

1. Unambitious women who are working because it's the thing to do and because they need some place to sit all day.

2. Unambitious men who are supporting themselves while they tackle the theater, television or the Great American Novel, mostly on company time.

3. Extremely ambitious men and women who feel that the Boss Lady's job is an easier target than a man's

would be and spend most of their energies trying to get it.

Men, as previously observed, are altogether underjoyed to work for women and usually do a deep burn at the very thought of taking orders, tactful directions, gentle suggestions or left-handed hints from a female employer—even if she signs their checks. The big exception: men who are superconfident of (a) their capabilities and (double-a) their own "manhood"—in brief, the ballsy types who are so sure of themselves that they never feel put down by anything.

These are the greatest men in the world—the ideal ones to have around in business situations, blizzards, flash fires or blackouts. One of them is Frank Pistone, an art director I've worked with for fourteen years. He has the sensitivity to be a crack designer, layout artist and colorist, and he is also loaded with muscle and macho. Frank is attracted to difficult and demanding situations and feels challenged by them on a personal basis. He got the Army's highest grade for field expediency in the course of surviving three days in a forest with no supplies except a fifteen-inch piece of string. It's beautiful to see his expediency in action, as he pushes a rented car through a snowstorm to get us to a meeting on time or puts together a million-dollar campaign to meet an impossible deadline. He loudly declares his attitude toward women to be "oldstyle Italian or old guinea uncle," but this seldom comes through in work situations. As his principal client I am, technically, the boss, but neither of us pays much attention to that—probably a major reason why we get along well. We give each other a very wide berth!

Between the extremes represented by Betty Shaver and Gertrude Ashtabula, I have had a number of lady bosses and learned something of value from all of them.

A few of them helped me do my best work, some actively prevented my doing anything of any consequence and at least one clearly didn't give a damn what I did or how well I did it as long as it didn't create any problems for her. When they were "good" bosses (that is, the kind who helped me and everybody else perform at the top of our capabilities), it was not because they were women. And when they were less than that, it was not because they were not men. The good ones might have had an easier time of it as men, but I'm not so sure about that either. Maybe they wouldn't have tried as hard to be effective or fair either.

While every test yet devised to measure human intellect has revealed no significant differences in the IQ of the sexes, there are still differences in attitudes that make positions of authority more difficult for women. As previously observed, authority is power, and its effects can be awesome. Being aware of this is important. Being aware of other people's reactions to it is even more so. Until gender attitudes undergo a tremendous change, any woman who accedes to power in business had better use it with more caution than enthusiasm. Above all, she cannot use it the same way she does in her own private little world, where she can resort to the little personal stratagems that work with family and friends because they love her or are, at least, tolerant of her "ways." In business, if things are to go as she wants them to, her approach should be marked by the kind of diplomacy and tact that may not be necessary around home base.

Any Boss Lady has a tough time adjusting to the people around her, whether they work for her or not. Workmen, suppliers, salesmen, clients and executives of other companies tend to assume that she's either an easy mark who can be readily exploited or such a bitch that she deserves to be duped. The men who work for her feel that she's going to give them a hard time because they're men, and the women feel that they're going to get it because they're women. Unless she's a real Ashtabula, she just feels like throwing up in her wastebasket.

I guess the best thing for a boss of either sex to remember is what it's like not to be one. The best ones I've had all seemed to understand the tenuous nature of the relationship and the two-way hazards involved. They treated everybody who worked for them as responsible adults, and it's difficult to respond to such treatment like anything else. I have a strong suspicion, too, that these good bosses were merely behaving toward their hirelings the way they preferred being treated themselves. Uneasy rests the head that wears a crown? Uneasy, also, rests the head that doesn't!

Burning the Evidence

I first became aware of my own ability to make things go my way when I was about four years old and under pressure from my mother to wear an expensive dress that had been bought for, and rejected by, my older sister. Mama was given to Olympian extravagances, an outgrowth of her belief that she had married a rich man. It was a belief Dad underlined by declaring himself so at least once a day and by indulging himself in extravagances that only a wealthy man could afford: oversized touring cars, custom-made shotguns, a bizarre collection of walking sticks (one of buffalo horn, others covered with exotic skins or inlaid with unlikely material such as wolves' teeth set in silver and turquoise), a kennel full of pedigreed hunting dogs, rare birds and fish, which he released in the nearby woods and rivers, and a 35-millimeter film projector that he used to screen Charlie

Chaplin comedies for anyone who cared to join him in the abandoned bakery building at the center of our movie-theaterless town.

Under the circumstances Mama felt free, even constrained, to buy clothes for my sister and me at Mme. Amalie's, an elegant little shop in the French Quarter in New Orleans, where everything was handmade. Louie's dress that she wanted me to wear had cost $45, the equivalent of at least $200 now, and hardly small change for a growing little girl's garment. It was smocked and embroidered with the typical abandon of the French —the sort of thing my sister usually adored—but it had promptly become an object of disgust to her because she had not participated in the choice.

The dress was not returnable. (No dummy, Mme. Amalie. Dad called her Madam No Quarter of the French Quarter.) And even a rich man's wife could feel guilty about a $45 dress hanging wastefully in the closet, unworn by an obstinate and ungrateful child. She therefore determined to alter the dress and press it into service on me, since I was younger and usually easier to get along with. But on this occasion I was equally determined. If Louie wouldn't wear it, neither would I. I was staging a raucous one-woman protest at the top of my talent when the pharaoh arrived on the scene.

"What the hell's wrong with Josie?" he asked.

"She doesn't want to wear this beautiful little dress!"

"Why not?"

"I got it for Louise and she won't have it! It was forty-five dollars at Mme. Amalie's, and it's never been worn even once!"

"Why won't Louie wear it?"

"She didn't pick it out."

"Why won't Josie wear it? Don't tell me. I know. For Christ's sweet sake—and mine!—throw it in the fire!"

With that he flung the offending garment onto the

102

flaming logs in the fireplace, and as I watched the despised brown velvet disappear in a merry flare of oranges, yellows and reds, I was choked with solid worship. At that moment my father became God—the omnipotent being who moved to set things right with swift finality (and damn the cost!), a holy presence capable of destroying dissension by fire. At the same moment a light bulb flashed on in my head: If he was God, what did that make me? After all, I had been chief catalyst in the scenario, hadn't I?

Extravagant as the gesture was, it was an act of genius because it was an unforgettably dramatic way to resolve a deadlock and, at the same time, to wipe the emotional slate clean for all concerned. Mama's guilt feelings, Louise's fury and my own festering sense of insult—all were burned to ashes before our very eyes.

What a pity that most business disagreements can't be settled so quickly and to such glowing satisfaction of all the disputants. The situation that Mama and Louise and I were in represented a classic cause of business strife: (a) Top management had made a costly mistake and was trying to "amortize" it; (b) a senior member of the team who might have averted the error was angry over not having been consulted; and (c) a junior member felt put down at being forced to bail out the other two.

Seeing my father turn arsonist in my behalf was lovely for my little ego, but one of the first things I learned in business is that what works at home doesn't play at the office. Men need and actively seek female approval—*at a personal level*—and will go to interesting lengths to get it from wives, daughters, sweethearts, mothers, even female in-laws. But by the time they get to the office they're so worn out with the demands and disagreements of their nearest and dearest, they're not about to put up with any more yammering or bossing from the women *here*. Not many offices keep roaring fires going in open fireplaces. And fewer still are manned by executives who are willing to stoke them with anybody's mistakes but their own.

What Works at Home Often Bombs at the Office

Confusion over their conflicted roles in a "liberated society" has sent working women off to psychiatrists in multitudes. Dr. Alexandra Symonds is associate clinical professor of psychiatry New York University College of Medicine, and training analyst at the American Institute of Psychoanalysis, Karen Horney Center in New York. Speaking at a recent meeting of the American Academy of Psychoanalysts, Dr. Symonds said this:

> The feminist movement has reached women in all walks of life, causing them to question attitudes, feelings and behavior which they formerly took for granted. They are not only questioning their attitudes but are actively seeking to change. Many are returning to school for more education. Young women are applying in large numbers for admission into professional schools such as law medicine and engineering. Women are now in executive positions in business, government and banking where they had never been before. All of this activity brings new problems.
>
> Those who are trying to take advantage of the new opportunities opening up are also required to make a characterological change from a predominantly compliant dependent personality to a more expansive one. This causes symptoms, anxieties, marital stress, and profound turmoil.
>
> For example it is not appropriate for an executive in a bank to break down in tears when her superior questions something she has done. It is not acceptable for a senior editor earning $30,000 a year to act "cute" and seductive when her plan is reject-

ed; or for a college professor to sulk because she has been given a poor schedule, hoping that the Dean will notice and change it. These are patterns acceptable for "Daddy's little girl" rather than a liberated woman acting autonomously. Nevertheless, each one of these events occurred to various patients of mine.

The tears, coyness and sulking that are thought of as the traditional weapons of "the weaker sex" are worse than ineffectual at the office. As Dr. Symonds suggests, these are not suitable behavior patterns for a grown woman who wants to be something more independent and autonomous than El Bosso's baby. I wouldn't dream of staging the kind of protest scene in business that set the stage for my father's grandiloquent gesture all those years ago at the family fireplace. But I often wish he were around to push a few people into the fire for reinforcing the ancient attitudes about women in business—people like Dr. Symonds' female patients who have reacted exactly the way men expect them to at the office. "Just like a woman!"

I have no doubt that the bank executive wept, or that the senior editor acted "cute" and seductive, or that the college professor sulked. But I have seen men react to business disappointments in precisely the same ways without having their behavior dismissed as male emotionalism. I once worked with a male vice-president who burst into tears so often that he became known as Weepin' Willie, with several others who could be counted on to exude wheedling, unctuous "charm" when their ideas were attacked and with a number of supersulkers who would cloud up and pout for days on end over matters too picayune to mention. Moreover, I have seen men at the office throw tantrums that would dishonor a six-year-old child, threatening physical injury and even death to whoever had dared to disagree with them. Yet as far as I know, none of them felt constrained to seek psychiatric help. And nobody said, "Just like a man!"

The fact that men in business frequently indulge in the same kind of emotional behavior that the entire female sex is accused of on a more or less permanent basis does not get women off the hook. We all hang there because historically, traditionally, culturally, we are pegged as the people who cry, turn coy and sulk on the job because we're "too emotional." When women overreact to frustrations in business, we are behaving in the context of second sexism, a lifetime of put-downs made up of little, impersonal slights and great, big, deadly personal insults. But any woman who thinks she can trade on "past injustices" to get what she wants at the office is in for another put-down. If she dares cry, turn coy or sulk, she is reinforcing the prejudice that every working woman most fervently wants wiped out. She is acting "just like a woman."

Getting and keeping the right kind of help aren't easy for anybody, and for the Boss Lady, the problem is compounded. It might simplify matters to remember the following things:

1. *The reluctance of men and women to work for a woman is more traditional than personal, and you shouldn't feel offended or affronted when you realize that you're no exception.*

2. *Nevertheless, do not hire people of either sex who are openly hostile to the idea of reporting to a Boss Lady.* Some women, new to the wonderful world of bossland, set out with the optimistic conviction that they can turn the most reluctant dragon into an enthusiastically cooperative lamb, and while this *can* happen—and occasionally does—it's self-defeating to burden yourself with the added chore of converting a nonbeliever.

3. *Do not bring your maternal instincts to the office.*

You're the boss there—not "somebody's mother." Treat the people who work for you like responsible adults, and they'll usually respond accordingly. Treat them like a pack of runny-nosed brats, and they'll probably act that way.

4. *Respect the talents and even the eccentricities of your employees, and they're more likely to respect your own.*

5. *Do not give orders when it is possible to arrive at a plan of action through discussion and mutual understanding.* Everybody balks at arbitrary decisions and the "orders" that come out of them—especially when they come from a woman.

6. *Since people will be expecting you to "act like a woman," avoid any behavior that can be labeled as such.* Men can get away with tears and tantrums on the grounds that they are concerned, warm human beings. Women who get upset and show it are said to be too "emotional."

8

"Just a Secretary"'"

In business the boss behind the boss is often the ninety-pound weakling who describes herself as "just a secretary." It has been said that secretaries run New York, an excessive statement but an interesting idea— one that contains a large enough kernel of truth to attract examination.

The secretaries do decide which letters and memos are whisked right in to the boss for immediate action and which are shuffled to the bottom of the stack, where they may catch his attention at the end of the day, the end of the week or maybe never. (I personally am overcome with admiration for the corporation head I've read about who goes to his headquarters three times a year, in the middle of the night, marches into the office of each of his executives and sweeps every piece of paper on every desk into the trash. His stated reason: Everybody is entitled to a fresh start now and then. The result: The shuffle stacks in his executive suite are small to nonexistent.)

"Just secretaries" decide which calls are shot through to Mr. Omnipotence immediately and which are put on hold until the caller gets a cauliflower ear or wearies of feeling like a living extension of the Bell System and hangs up. New Yorkers enjoy repeating the story (perhaps apocryphal)about two executive secretaries whose bosses were on fire to talk to each other about a big deal they were maneuvering but were unable to hold a conversation because neither secretary would put her boss on the line first. This was the old game of secretarial one-upmanship: *"My* boss is more important than *your* boss. Tell yours to pick up the phone, and when he's on the line, I'll buzz Mr. Omnipotence. Not before."

When the bosses are out of town, out to lunch all afternoon or tied up in one of those never-ending meetings, their secretaries "keep the show on the road," fielding a lot of flak that their illustrious employers handle personally when they're on the scene. The good secretaries, of course, have studied the terrain and general management style. They understand how their employers operate and can take over an enormous amount of detail that probably should be delegated anyway. These women have the ideal vantage point for learning the business from the inside out, and they quickly catch onto the big company secrets, little personal secrets and all the other juicy stuff that takes some of the tedium out of typing and filing.

Once a Secretary, Always a Secretary—Says Who?

Many job counselors join militant feminists in vociferously advising career-minded young women not to learn secretarial skills. Although I do not agree with this advice, I can understand the reasoning behind it. Too often the reward for being a crack secretary is the opportunity to remain a crack secretary, but the smarter ones recognize the job as a handy-dandy way to learn all there is to know about a department, a division, a company or a whole conglomerate.

It is true that until recently young men applying for jobs were almost never asked if they could type, but equally true that a lot of them started out in the mail room, in the shipping department or maybe driving a company truck. Now some of them even start out typing —and taking shorthand. McGraw-Hill, publisher of the

Gregg shorthand books, keeps a record of important businessmen (as well as women) who learned shorthand in their youth and have continued to use it for their own purposes after becoming standout successes in their chosen fields. One of these is a present associate of mine, David Inouye, a brilliant marketing research specialist, who went to business school "to get off the farm." He quickly picked up shorthand, took notes with it at Harvard Business School and has continued to use it to great advantage throughout his career.

It should be noted here that male secretaries are now much in demand and have become a status symbol among female executives. This may be a subconscious dramatization of the role reversal, or even a conscious one. Some women clearly get a large charge out of pressing the buzzer and saying, "Come in please, Henry—and bring your pad." And Henry doesn't seem to mind. Male secretaries are still so scarce and the demand for them is so newly heavy that law or no law, their employment opportunities seem to be more equal than the girl's. Henry doesn't have to have good legs either.

Galling though it may be to be expected to type, file and answer telephones to get into a desirable job situation in a sexist world, young women may take comfort in the knowledge that they couldn't possibly be in a better spot to learn a whole business. If the only way you can get a shot at the kind of work you really want to do is to offer up a few office skills as your entrance fee, my advice to you is to do it. As the song goes, "It Ain't What You Do, It's the Way That You Do It." An impressive number of business biggies started out doing rock-bottom jobs.

One of the best secretaries I ever knew worked for a man I'll call Jud Harrigan, a key executive of a major food-processing company. Jud was several years beyond the company's retirement age but had been urged to stay

110

on because he was pure wizard at his job—in spite of the fact that he habitually lunched on six to eight ounces of warm gin and a handful of cocktail onions at one or more of the local watering holes. He said the onions were good for his liver.

I always tried to arrange my appointments with Jud for three o'clock in the afternoon, when he was most entertaining—just after he had finished the gin-and-onion repast and returned to the office to answer the day's memos, a stream of trivia which he looked upon as an affront to human intelligence, and waste of everybody's time. He would buzz Connie and ask her to bring in a pad for dictation, and she dutifully did. With a straight face and an entirely businesslike manner she would commit his replies to flawless shorthand. They were never more than thirty words long, and they usually went like this:

Replying to your request of April 10th that I outline my plans for the introduction of our new product in San Francisco, you bet your sweet ass I won't. Faithfully, Judson K. Harrigan.

Re: Your memo of April 10th. Incredible. Did a grown man write this or has your grandson taken over the correspondence in your office? The six-year-old? Faithfully, Ming Toy Harrigan Levy.

Julian—I know you can't help it but try. You are an insufferable sonofabitch and everything you write me proves it. Desist! Desist! Desist! Harrigan.

Attention: Charles S. Benderwall. Leave me alone. I'm an old man. JKH.

Connie would type up the memos like lightning, bring them in for his signature, thank him crisply and retire to the processing room, where she dumped all of them into the paper shredder. Then she'd go back to her desk, type new memos containing the information that the incoming batch had requested and get his signature on the revised versions. Connie and Jud both enjoyed the charade, and neither ever mentioned it.

I wish I could report that when Jud finally did retire, Connie moved into his job, but it didn't happen. However, when the promotion didn't materialize for her, Jud recommended her to another food company, and she is now public relations director there.

A secretary can, of course, speed you along toward the giddying heights of your organization or catapult you into a soft-walled room in a nice locked-up rest home. In a large corporation you may not have the luxury of choosing your own secretary and thereby casting your own dice between stardom and therapy rest. Owing to government regulations, corporate policy, company politics and a lot else, the keeper of the keys to your business fate may come to you through the courtesy and wisdom of Personnel, where they know what's best for you, even if they don't know what you're doing, how it's done and what could possibly help you do it. Or your secretary may be delivered to you by your own beloved boss, who is hell-bent on hanging onto every little detail of hiring and firing as a matter of personal muscle flexing and a means of building lower-echelon loyalty.

The latter happened to me when I was a copywriter and group supervisor at a mammoth advertising agency. I was not "big" enough to have a secretary, but in the pecking order I did rate a copy typist, and that's how Roselle came into my life. She was hired by the administrative head of our department, who was so eager to exercise her hiring prerogative that she sped Roselle onto the payroll without pausing to test her typing.

Roselle was a brilliant girl, but there were extenuating circumstances—lots of them. For one thing, she couldn't type. And for another, she was easily the most unabashed liar I ever met. She had sworn in the job interview that she could type ninety words a minute without error, when the actuality was that she was hard pressed to find the space bar on any typewriter. She explained to me that the IBM Selectric she was expected to use was "spooky" and insisted that when she touched it, she could hear a child weeping—probably her little brother, she said, who had died in a fire, by drowning, under the hooves of a runaway horse or in a train wreck, depending on Roselle's whim at any given moment.

My immediate superior, a woman who wanted to be consulted about *every*thing, was furious because she hadn't been involved in selecting personnel for her area. But she didn't want to be disagreeable because she was on the brink of a big promotion. So who got stuck with a copy typist who couldn't type? As junior member of the team, outranked by all the reigning warriors, I did.

In most businesses it is death to pick a dud for employment by one's firm at any level, and to cover the error in judgment, the dud picker will resort to any stratagem short of killing the incompetent and disposing of the body in a barrel of quick lime. Since women in key spots feel extremely vulnerable (because they often are), the dud picker in this case would have seen us all in hell, typing our own pearly prose at ten words a minute, before she would have admitted a hiring mistake—especially since she hadn't paused to give Roselle the customary typing test.

Result: stalemate. The untyped copy piled up while I listened to Roselle's ever more fanciful accounts of her little brother's demise. The day she told me that he might not be dead at all, that a neighbor had seen him picked up by a flying saucer, I decided that an imagination like that should be rechanneled. I split my assignments with

113

her, cutting my own work load 50 percent, and used the spare time teaching her to write copy—no chore at all because she was a great natural. She was so good, in fact, that it was a cinch to slip her into the next opening we had for a copywriter. I was rewarded with a crackerjack typist who had taken the test and had no dead brothers weeping inside the IBM Selectric. And Roselle, I am happy to say, parlayed her failure at the typewriter into dazzling success as an ad writer. Everybody was happy about the whole thing—especially the woman who had hired her without testing her typing skills. She still boasts that she gave Roselle her first big chance. So does the division head who wanted her fired. And so do I!

Don't Forget Your Kid Gloves

Secretaries often have tremendous clout, born not only of skill and judgment but also of knowledge of where the bodies are buried. The smarter executives understand this and cultivate their favor, taking care never to ask them to fetch an ashtray or place a phone call for them. They treat Mr. Omnipotence's secretary much the same way they treat Mr. O. himself and try not to tremble in the process. It is widely assumed that it is easier for male executives to cultivate the high-level secretaries than it is for their female associates, but this is not necessarily the case. Women executives can show secretaries special consideration—and should. This not only can help keep the lines of communication open to Mr. O., Mr. Semi-O., et al., but can go a long way toward quelling any envy that springs in the secretarial breast at the sight of another woman in a position of power.

A female vice-president in the detergent industry told me that she goes out of her way to "be nice" to her own secretary, as well as to the secretaries of other executives in the company. "There is, of course, a status structure among secretaries," she said. "Any good executive secretary wants to work for the most powerful person in the company that she can, and since the men at our place have, until recently, had all the power, my secretary at first felt marked down to be working for a woman. I knew that she had lost face with the other secretaries when she was assigned to me, although she kept a stiff upper lip about it. Very stiff! She 'cooperated' because she'd been around long enough to play the company game, but I could tell by that upper lip that her heart wasn't in it. So at Christmastime I arranged for her to be hostess at an elegant luncheon for all the other executive secretaries. The party was at one of the 'in' restaurants, and it was her show all the way. She signed the check by an arrangement I had previously made with the maître d', and I, of course, wasn't there. This promptly lent new cachet to her job and gave her an entirely different attitude toward both my status and hers. She no longer feels marked down; rather, she feels a bit privileged and unique, so her cooperation is now a beautiful, smiling thing!"

The woman who told me this added that she makes a point of being friendly to *all* the secretaries—never aloof or condescending—because they are inclined to resent the fact that some woman other than themselves has a corporate title and all that goes with it. They manage, largely, to forgive the men for having these rewards, but the sight of them accruing to a member of their own sex is a bit much.

"If I were cool to these women," she says, "they might give me a hard time in ways I wouldn't even know about, so I treat them with consideration and respect. I listen closely when they speak to me confidentially about a business matter—especially when they fling me a few quick words, sotto voce, when I'm on my way to a meeting. I know that the secretary doing this is trying to influence me on behalf of her boss, but what she says may give me some valuable insights. I'm glad to get the tipoff before the matter comes up because I gain precious time to think it through and decide whether her boss is about to be a hero or a bum. It's better politics to vote with the heroes. . . ."

Here are some notes for both Boss Ladies and secretaries. For the Boss Lady:

1. *Hire the smartest secretaries you can, and make it worthwhile for them—with money and/or the opportunity to learn and advance.*

2. *Delegate responsibility to them.* Provide them with all the information and backing they need to act in your behalf. If you can't trust them, fire them, and if you can trust them, reward them.

3. *Treat them with consideration and respect.* The fact that a person in your office is younger and less experienced than you are or has a job with a less lofty title than you do does not confer any special superiority on you. The secretaries may be smarter than you are—as many a one has proved.

4. *If they have other ambitions, don't try to keep them nailed to a typewriter no matter how much you need them there.* They won't stay there anyway, and you'll only be wasting time and effort.

For the secretary:

1. *If your boss is a woman, do not assume that her gender has somehow jellied her brain.* She may be more gifted and capable than the men you wish you worked for.

2. *Do not feel demeaned by having to do typing and filing as long as you're learning other things.* Pay attention to everything you type and file because it may turn out to be as important to you as it is to the company.

3. *Make your ambitions and plans known to your employer, and if they're not achievable there, move on.*

Reasonable employers will understand this, and unreasonable ones don't matter.

4. *Be as nice to the other people in the office as you are to the boss.* It makes the day go faster, and you never know who'll be doing what tomorrow—or writing your next reference.

9
Shut Up and Listen—You May Learn Something

Fair or not, women have the reputation for being the talkative sex. All of us know men whose compulsive gabble makes Muhammad Ali and Howard Cosell appear to be a pair of mutes. We know women, too, who are as silent as Garbo. It's no matter. Despite the examples of Ali, Cosell and Garbo, the female sex has not won blanket license to prattle away at the office like a gaggle of geese on speed.

Radio and television have taught us all to hate and fear "dead air." Since every second on the electronic media is a potential revenue producer calculated in cold, hard cash, the stations have decreed that something has to be happening at each and every tick of the studio clock, from sign-on till "The Star-Spangled Banner." Let there be sound. Let there be action. Let there be anything, Lord, but silence. For at the networks, silence is in no way golden. It is lost money, lost audience, lost face.

When a talk show guest suddenly clams up (out of vodka paralysis or a sudden attack of self-consciousness), when a nearsighted star picks up the wrong pair of glasses and can't read a word of the script, when the teleprompter gets screwed up and the whole cast loses the place and nothingness sets in, it's a disaster. Everybody at the station goes crazy, and the audience, long accustomed to nonstop sound and motion, may be seized with similar paroxysms of panic. Is another power failure on the way, another blackout? Are the creatures from Mars landing at last in New Jersey?

Attitudes nurtured by radio and television make silence all the more deafening, and women feel constrained to *do something* about it. Having been brought up on the belief that life's little amenities are their special responsibility, they feel that it's up to them not only to "keep the conversation going" but to steer it into placid channels when disagreements crop up.

The woman who has already become a Boss Lady knows that differences of opinion can be good for business, that they can help "get the bugs out" of a plan or an idea before it's put into action. She can, however, still fall into the trap of prattling. Feeling tenuous about her position, she may tittle away about trivia to avoid committing herself on an important matter or to sidestep a premature decision. Men frequently stall for time this way, but they're not the sex with the reputation for talking things up.

My father couldn't stand small talk or much talk of any kind unless he was doing it. He habitually sat at the cash register in his supershabby restaurant in Mississippi, reading and fervently hoping that no one would say anything to him. He despised the restaurant and did everything he could to alienate the customers—especially the ones who interrupted his reading. I remember seeing him charge a man $1.90 for a cup of coffee, back when coffee was a nickel almost everywhere. He was sitting at the cash register that day reading Edgar Allan Poe when an out-of town innocent, who had just downed a cup of coffee at the counter, approached. When Dad didn't look up the customer rapped a nickel sharply on the glass top of the cigar case. Still not looking up from his book, Dad said, "Yes. What is it? Did the dam break?"

"How much do I owe for a cup of coffee?" the man asked.

"That'll be a dollar ninety," Dad said, unfolding his six-foot-four frame and standing up to display more than two hundred pounds of physical power.

"A *dollar ninety!*" was the outraged protest. "Why, everybody knows a cup of coffee's a nickel, all over the world."

"Yeah," Dad said. "Everybody knows that. And that's why you're going to pay me a dollar and ninety cents. A nickel for the coffee, eighty-five cents for making that racket on the cigar case when I've got a splitting headache and a dollar for interrupting Edgar Allan Poe. Pay me or I'll kill you."

The customer quickly counted out $1.90 and fled, muttering to himself about crazy people, Mississippi and his determination never to set foot in the state again. Dad turned and adjusted a sign on the wall behind him. The sign read:

Far better to remain silent and be thought a fool than to speak and remove all doubt.—Anonymous

I never knew whether the gesture with the sign was meant for the customer or himself. Maybe he meant it for me. At any rate, I have tried to remember it in tense business situations where it's difficult to keep quiet. Executive women feel that they're under the gun to make a contribution, and this can cause the most reticent ones among us to express an opinion or make a suggestion before enough facts have been developed for anybody to have a valid response. This, of course, goes on all the time in the male camp, too, but either it sounds worse when we do it or seems to.

So if you're not sure of your ground, don't try to cover it up by pontificating on and around the subject or by switching gears altogether and filling your listener in on the details of a movie you saw last week. Feel free to say quickly and simply that you'd like to think the matter through a little further before giving an opinion. If you're pressed for immediate answers, say that something has come up which may change your mind, and if the operator of the pressure cooker you're in asks, "What?" just smile and add, "I'll get back to you." You're entitled.

If you haven't yet made it to the upper reaches of your company, it's still a good idea to go with the Garbo school. The troops who come to work mainly to hear, spread and start the daily latrine rumors won't like you much for this, but management will.

Maybe There's Gold in the Garbage

One of the most valuable habits you can cultivate is listening, quietly, attentively, patiently. Learn to listen between the lines to what is *not* being said because the omissions sometimes tell you more than the spoken words. Granted that a lot of what you hear will be drivel, misinformation and mental garbage, but it's still useful to know the principal sources of that kind of stuff, too. Don't let anything start you talking to keep from listening. Buried in there somewhere may be the nucleus of an idea that can make money for the company, enhance corporate prestige and score a few extra Brownie points for you.

Office gossip, like death and taxes, is always with us. Listen, but don't give out any tidbits in return. I once escaped from an unfavorable lease because Jeanette Connolly, who works with me as office manager, was listening but not talking in the ladies' room.

We were unhappy in the building where our offices were located. The elevators were maddeningly slow, and the cleaning services were sloppy. And we learned the hard way that the security was nonfunctioning when every office machine we owned was stolen, a spectacular feat since the only exits were past points manned by "guards." The building manager was deeply sympathetic and said he'd be happy to let us break the lease by "buying it up"—that is, paying rent for the full term.

Meanwhile, in the ladies room Jeanette heard an employee from the firm next door complain that her offices were overcrowded, that her management was desperate for more space and would be glad when "those people moved." Those people were us. Armed with this information, we were able to negotiate a lease break that saved us $20,000—or the inconvenience of staying on.

What you hear in the course of office gossip will seldom be worth $20,000, but it's always a good idea to be alert and aware of whatever is happening. The woman who becomes a Boss Lady learns how to sift out the trivial stuff and hang onto the few nuggets.

Every simpleminded how-to book you read pounds you with the importance of being a good listener, assuring you that an open ear can win you a reputation for being one of the world's great conversationalists. If that's what you never wanted to be, hear this: It can win you a reputation for being a sound executive until that great day when you actually are. Just keep your mouth shut until you're reasonably sure you know what the hell you and all the others are talking about.

Naturally a reputation for being a sympathetic listener can make you an easy mark for the resident time killers—all the company malcontents, the garrulous types enchanted with the sound of their own voices and the ever-undecided souls who enjoy Jesuitical debate on every little point of a given project. You can protect yourself from these people in several ways: (a) Make it clear at the start of the conversation that you have just X minutes, and at the end of that time, unless something vital is surfacing, look at your watch, apologize briefly and move along swiftly. (b) Get yourself a tiny desk clock with an alarm that buzzes audibly but not loudly enough to give you a nervous collapse. Set it for a given length of time, and when it sounds, that's it. There's something about the ring of an alarm that impresses everybody, and you can end the interview definitely but gracefully with a quick apology the moment it goes off. (c) Alert your secretary to come in at a certain time or to get on the intercom with the news that it's time for your meeting or your call to, say, Houston. If Houston or wherever stirs memories or sparks a thought in your talkative visitor, you can just say something gracious and firm about discussing it later.

Even the conversation lovers can grow weary of their overloquacious peers. For several years I worked with a woman I'll call Beatrice Frye. Beatrice was as brilliant as she thought she was but not smart enough to stop talking about it. Somehow she managed to spend at least two hours of every day roaming the corridors, telling anyone she could collar about her latest coup. And Beatrice had coups the way the cat has kittens—in litters and distressingly often. It usually didn't matter to her whether anyone appeared to be concentrating on her tales of triumph or not. She would be so absorbed in the joy of reliving her victories that she hardly noticed the inattentiveness of her target audience. On other occasions, however, when she felt that her victory was especially worthy of note, she would turn on the group she had approached and bellow, "Are you listening to me or talking among yourselves?"

Management heard her in spite of the fact that everybody else had learned to give her the deaf-ear treatment. And although she had abundant intellectual equipment, she was repeatedly passed over for promotions and eventually fired. There were at least three other vice-presidents on the premises with oral diarrhea as uncontrolled as hers. But they were men.

People have been talking when they ought to have been listening ever since prehistoric grunts became intelligible speech. Look at it this way: When you're talking, if you're not just filling in dead air you're giving out information; when you're listening, you at least have a chance to take in something. And in business it is more blessed to receive information than to give it out—until you're ready to apply it in the right places.

Everybody who has an ounce of career ambition is on one end or the other of a practice repulsively known as brain picking. It stands to reason that it is more rewarding to be a picker than pickee, although it can certainly be ego-massaging to show off what you know. It is even considered acceptable form for a caller to exclaim with high ebullience, "Hey, how about letting me drop in for a moment or maybe buy your lunch? I want to pick your brains!" Compliment, right? Right! But just remember that the pickings are worth money, and you're not obligated to scatter them across the grass for anyone except the people who pay you for what you know. Women used to be particularly vulnerable to the brain-picking ploy, but most of them are now catching on to the axiom of their most successful male associates: "Don't tell anybody anything they can use before you do, better than you do—or against you!"

Won't that kind of attitude make you look like a dummy? Sure. To some people. But to the ones who matter, you'll look very wise.

Turn That Volume Down—or Off!

In their zeal to get attention, be listened to, invoke authority, women sometimes resort to volume, forgetting that the female voice, turned up, can sound very unpleasant. When it is also under stress, it can be all but unbearable. Noise can and does destroy. It has been demonstrated by serious scientists that ultrahigh levels of sound can actually set fire to the fur on a rat's back. Their experiments have also shown that exposing rats, mice and rabbits to noise stress over protracted periods of time can produce convulsions, liver atrophy and testicular degeneration in males.

This bit of information troubled me when I worked with Suellen Myers, who had an extremely strident voice that she made no audible effort to control. I felt a degree of concern about the flaming rat fur, not out of any deep sympathy for the rats, but because at the time I had a coat trimmed with an inelegant fur that I thought might be threatened. It had been my custom to hang the coat in a closet between my office and Suellen's, but after reading about the noise-ignited rats, I stopped keeping it there, being worried that the collar and cuffs would be singed off by Suellen's vocalizing.

When anything happened to displease her—which was almost any little thing that did happen—Suellen would pound out of her office like Billy Martin erupting from the dugout bent on killing the umpire, and go into her war dance. She would shriek at top volume, above high C and off the scale, until any opposition had subsided and all adversaries, real or imagined, had either collapsed at her feet or fled. The men were usually terrified, a reaction she relished, but this was eventually just what did her in. Our male associates did not feel warm and happy to have women around in positions of importance anyway, and Suellen's raucous responses to everyday problems gave them an acceptable reason for condemning the female invasion. (Didn't this prove that women are disruptive?) Suellen, who was the highest-ranking woman on the premises, was fired, and the rest of us found ourselves in corporate limbo.

Men at work get especially annoyed when they are bombarded with conversation while they are trying to solve a problem or just engaged in some deep worrying about a problem that, in all probability, can't be solved. I once saw Ed Gray, an advertising executive with a courtly manner toward both sexes, suppress the urge to strangle two women at a critical moment. The two kept badgering him with "advice" while he was waiting for a client to come in and fire the agency that we all worked for. Said client controlled an account which brought the agency an annual income of more than half a million dollars, and Ed, whose responsibility it was to keep the income in the house, might be described as momentarily devastated by the impending loss.

I was on the team recruited for a last-ditch effort to save the account. As the account director in charge Ed was to make the agency's final presentation, in prayerful hope that it would not be final. While we were waiting, these two women copywriters regularly assigned to the account arrived for the meeting and undertook to advise Ed on how to handle the hairy matter. Their advice: March in and preserve the agency's dignity by telling the client to take his account and shove it! That must have been what Ed ached to do. But I know of no advertising agency that values its "dignity" more than half a million dollars a year. I know some whose principals profess to, but when the chips are down, few men or women at the top of any business will tell a customer to shove half a million dollars a year. That is a copywriter's dream, not a business executive's reality.

Ed was courteous to his talkative advisers, but sparing their tactics, he took a conciliatory approach to the irate client. And his presentation was so effective that he managed to pull our dignity out of the fire along with the account. We kept both, though I'll never know how he got his thoughts together during the premeeting barrage.

Please—No Shoptalk! Enough, Already

Women who are excited by their jobs frequently get so carried away that they take the excitement into other areas of their lives and talk shop to people who are, (a) uncomprehending, (b) envious or (c) not the faintest bit interested. Women who do not work outside the home usually respond to this line of gab with (a) bewilderment, (b) irritation or (c) simple boredom—unless they're planning to go out and get a job themselves. Men subjected to shoptalk by a woman are likely to flee as if a hungry grizzly had suddenly attacked. It is safest to assume that only Mother is as fascinated as you are with what goes on at your office, and even she might prefer that you take her out to a good movie.

Talking shop is usually a kind of conversation that should be limited to exchanges with people in one's own field, and even that calls for discretion. I have a friend (a woman) who has an executive position with a company engaged in oil exploration. Another woman who has a minor job in the same industry drops in several times a week to chatter about oil leases, oil prices, drilling rigs, the Arabs, Congress and anything else that makes her feel importantly connected to a vital topic. My friend usually accepts the aural barrage with glassy-eyed patience. "I just give her a huge hello and a double-huge good-bye," she says. "She's harmless but sometimes exasperating. Once, when she was telling me a story that seemed as long as the *Encyclopaedia Britannica,* I made the mistake of asking her an innocent question—only to be polite. She gave me a condescending smile and an amazing reply. She said, 'Frances, I'm sorry. We don't give out that kind of information in the oil business!' "

Men can drive women crazy with shoptalk, too, but this apparently doesn't occur to them. I have stopped going to a restaurant I really like because the owner, knowing that I am in the advertising business, comes over to my table and reads me the ads he's written about his steaks. They're excellent ads, and I enjoy reading them in the local press. I might enjoy hearing him read them on other occasions. But when I go into a restaurant, I am there to relax and forget about the advertising business —unless I am with a client, and then he will surely be concerned with the promotion of his own products, not the great New York steak wars.

Although the sound of one's own voice may be the sweetest music this side of Lincoln Center, the world and our own little plots of it in particular would probably be better if we'd shut up and listen more often. It boils down to this:

1. *Silence IS golden, no matter what they say at CBS and your friendly local disco.* As noise pollution rises, so does the premium on quiet. Please do not disturb the peace at the office any more than it is disturbed already.

2. *While "thinking out loud" may help you crystallize your own ideas, this may also keep other people from crystallizing theirs.* Since theirs can do you as much good

as your own—maybe even more than yours—make your conversation an exchange, not a monologue.

3. *Do not let people outside your organization pick your brains unless they're good friends—or willing to pay.* What you know is worth money. Why give it away for the sake of a little ego trip?

4. *Don't speak up at a meeting until you have something meaningful to contribute.* Talking to attract attention may call attention only to your blank spots.

5. *Do not interrupt busy or worried people with gratuitous advice and comment.* Do not present them with any problem or idea that can wait.

6. *Never, never under any circumstances talk when you don't know what you're talking about.* This is the most obvious dictum in business, yet it remains the one most often violated.

7. *When you do speak, control the volume.* The female voice under stress can be an extremely unpleasant sound. It's hard to remember this when you're angry, upset or excited, but try to keep your voice down.

10

Those Little Male Gallantries — Trick or Treat?

Should a gentleman rise when a lady breezes into the boardroom? And if so, how should she react to the noble gesture? Do the rules of etiquette still apply at the office? Or is the whole game of "ladies and gentlemen" over?

The new woman, liberated and dashing in her role as executive or executive-candidate, often does not take well to the treatment she gets from men, in or out of the office. Maybe she looks as if she prefers a man-to-man climate. Maybe she has even said so. But when the chips are down, this may not be the case. I have seen more than one woman risk physical injury to herself and others to avoid preceding a man into a revolving door when he has stepped aside with an after-you-Alphonse gesture. Then I have heard the same woman complain that George, Bill or Frank has "poor business manners" because George, Bill or Frank neglected to stand when she entered an office.

Maybe that makes sense to some women, but it's understandably difficult for men to put these two conflicting attitudes together. Undeniably there are women among us who want it both ways, even as bosses—who want to be treated as independent equals in some instances and as lofty creatures entitled to special respect and deference in others. It's all right to want it, but don't expect it. The men are confused nowadays. As little boys a lot of them had the living daylights whaled out of them for "improper conduct" toward little girls, so they went to work prepared to use their best dancing school manners in the presence of anyone female, regardless of age, rank or income. Mario Marone, an art director I work with, told me about springing to his feet one day when an executive woman pounded into his office only to have her order him to "sit down before I knock you down." He said it unnerved him so completely that he has been sitting down ever since.

Granted. Some men do use those charming little gallantries to underline the fact that the women at the office are, after all, just girls—the weaker sex in need of male protection, care and assistance. How can a woman be expected to run a department if she can't even hail a cab or put her coat on without help? Still other men use such inflated gestures of courtesy to mask their hostility toward women—especially executive women. I once hired a young man who turned out to be a leaper. He would leap across a room with the agility of a trapeze artist to open a door for me—and then manage somehow to trip me as I went through it. He would also leap to hold my coat for me, starting out with the elaborate formality of a cloak-room attendant, then blocking one sleeve in such a way that I couldn't possibly put an arm through it without resorting to a battering ram. I, of course, wound up thrashing around the room like the most awkward kid in the third grade. After a couple of these frantic coat bouts with him I became convinced that the foul-up was no accident, and thereafter, when he leaped to hold my coat, I thanked him warmly but said, "Please, let me. This coat has a weird lining, and I can handle it better solo." I also remembered to go through doorways with a very gingerly step when he was standing at attention beside them.

In most companies where women are now actively in the running for executive jobs, competition between the sexes has been so combative that male courtesy has been virtually suspended. The attitude of the men seems to be: "You want to be free? Okay. Now that you're free to compete with me you're also free to follow me through doors, get onto elevators after I do, light your own Forest Lawn menthols and, if all the seats are taken at a meeting, sit on the bloody floor."

Some of the women—especially the younger ones— prefer it this way. "I'd much rather have Harry's job," says food executive Joan Freed, "than the chair he might get up and give me at some stupid meeting. The only chair I really want is the one behind his desk, and he knows it. So good old Harry just sits there like Lincoln's statue when I walk in and continues to sit even if all the seats are occupied. One of these days he's going to realize that I'm a lot more visible standing up—and that I appear more authoritative, too!"

Others, however, resent the revised office manners of the men and cite them as further evidence of chauvinistic piggery. "Whatever happened to common courtesy? And simple human decency?" complains a young woman in the cosmetic industry. "The men around here never lift a finger to help me do anything. You'd think they were all raised in a barn!" This young woman declares that she is independent, self-sufficient, inner-directed and self-propelled. All indications are that she really is. But when pressed, she admits that she enjoys having men dance attendance on her and doesn't understand why she's denied the compliment at the office.

Gee, Thanks—Even If You Don't Mean It

No matter how the Boss Lady feels about it personally, it isn't a good idea for her to make a big deal of male courtesy—or lack of it—in today's emotional climate. The wiser executive women I know accept the little male gallantries politely and matter-of-factly when they're offered and pay no attention when they're not. In either event it's asinine to make a scene. Men constantly extend courteous little gestures to each other and sometimes skip them altogether, with little thought being given to the matter either way. Smart women play it by ear, the same as they do.

Occasionally the Boss Lady may find herself in a sensitive situation with the restaurant check when she's entertaining a male client or a male associate whom she has invited to lunch or dinner. Although more and more men are willing—indeed, delighted!—for a woman to pay the bill, there are some Neanderthal types who go into paroxysms of embarrassment when it happens. If you're the woman who did the inviting and have the faintest inkling that your guest may be uncomfortable when the check hits the table, don't let it! Take the man to your club, where he can't pay. Or take him to a restaurant where you have a charge account and an understanding with the maître d'. When your secretary makes the reservation, ask her to say that there's to be no check on the table and the waiter is to add the tip. (But be sure to specify the percentage of the tip or you may get a rude shock.) And don't forget the maître d'—he's a man to keep buttered up, and this should be done as quietly and privately as possible.

Even if your guest seems completely at ease with the situation, it's better to use your charge account or credit card than cash. The most secure man this side of Prince Charles can start squirming when you start waving real money around. Also, if wine is in order, ask your male guest to pick it, and when he consults you about your preferences, don't feel constrained to tell him everything you know about the cabernet sauvignons familiar only to you and the house taster at Sherry-Lehmann.

Neither should you run a chemical analysis of the sauces on your own educated palate. You're not Gael Greene, there to review the restaurant and dazzle the whole room with your expertise. In short, don't try to show off just because you're paying the check. It will only mark you either as a neophyte who hasn't been in many first-class restaurants or as an incurable showoff.

Most of the executive women I know who are at ease with their status don't act like Donald Duck when they are addressed as Miss rather than Ms. or when somebody uses one of those enclitic little words like "chairman" instead of "chairperson." However, I do know a few high-level women who make king-size issues (correction—monarch-size issues) of these trivialities. To me, it isn't worth the effort. I understand the philosophy of wiping out sexism in the language, but in my opinion, getting yourself called Ms. won't make you chairman of the board any faster, and once there, getting yourself called chairperson won't give you any more clout.

Even if you're president, chairman or chairperson, even if you own the business lock, stock and notes at the bank, taking yourself superseriously can spoil the fun. Once, sometime after I went into business for myself, I spotted tarnish on a little silver candy dish in my office and impetuously took it into the john, where I was scrubbing away at it with silver polish when a militant young secretary from another office in our building walked in. She viewed the scene with surpassing disgust.

"Your boss has his fucking nerve!" she announced. Since I am ostensibly boss, I was thoroughly nonplussed.

"Why do you say that?" I asked her.

"Secretaries aren't supposed to polish silver," she said. "Only dummies and maids do that!"

"I'll tell him when he comes in," I said and fled.

Leave It to the Boys

That secretary's liberated rhetoric is fairly common among women at the office now, and it's interesting to see some of the male reactions to it. Of course, women have used these indelicate little Anglo-Saxonisms to each other for years, and men have felt perfectly free to use them to anyone they pleased, male or female, especially since World War II. At the office they have sometimes used them as a weapon against women and have cited "man talk" as a reason for excluding women from meetings, company social gatherings and whole job areas. Some men "blue up" the air in an effort to frighten Miss Muffet away, hoping that a steady outpour of obscenity will discourage the girls who are competing with them for jobs. In fairness, it must be said that women at the office often wither men the same way. Now that the girls are into barracks-type talk, the men often profess shock and horror, and I believe that some of them really are profoundly shocked and horrified. It has been said that one reason the troops opened fire on the students at Kent State was that coeds in the march were goading the young national guardsmen with inflammatory remarks expressed in sexual terms. Some of the men in the Guard, rural types, had never heard women talk like that and couldn't stand being taunted by beautiful young girls with words they considered obscene. Confused, angry, emotionally upset by the situation they opened fire. This is not to excuse them for their action, but to point out that men do react emotionally and even violently when they hear "man talk" tripping off the tongues of people who aren't men at all.

The double standard in verbiage surfaced most dramatically shortly after President Nixon (remember *him?*) appointed Helen Delich Bentley to serve as chairman of the Federal Maritime Commission. The incident was front-paged and broadcast all over the world, partly because the press was involved. While awaiting Senate confirmation of her appointment, Bentley took a little trip on the icebreaker SS *Manhattan,* covering the ship's historic voyage through the Northwest Passage to Alaska as maritime editor of the *Baltimore Sun.* She broke the ice but good. Transmitting a story to her newspaper via the ship's radio, she said an "ugly word" while the Coast Guard listened. Although the Coast Guard is bound to have heard everything on that radio, which must have included salty language uttered by other reporters, the reaction to Bentley's expletive was immediate and electric. All press people were summarily banished from the ship's voice communications.

Bentley told it this way: "I just used a common Anglo-Saxon expletive to express my impatience with a rewrite man, and lo and behold, the Federal Communications Commission bars all newsmen from communicating by voice with their offices."

It is not surprising that the chairman got the press gagged by talking like a charwoman. The only astonishing part was her own "lo and behold" reaction. One wonders how she traveled so far, all the way from her pretty pink cradle to the Northwest Passage, before discovering that there is, indeed, a double language—that words are male and female according to the sex of the user.

Ascribing gender to words in a way that linguists never intended has always seemed ridiculous to me. Also: why should we damn some of them as obscene while we bestow on others the questionable blessing of propriety? If one word is "dirty," how can half a dozen others denoting exactly the same article or action possibly be "clean"? Theory abounds. One holds that at least some of the monosyllabic Anglo-Saxonisms are distinct onomatopoeia—verbal duplication of bodily sounds that traditionally are entitled to privacy. But I'll leave that kind of fruitless speculation to the social scientists and the linguists.

My own vocabulary was ripened, if not enriched, by a backslid Baptist father who frequently expressed himself with more color than decorum. Listening to the ease and spontaneity of his controversial speech, I became hooked on the notion that there is majesty, even poetry, in an imaginatively conceived and emotionally delivered stream of profanity-cum-obscenity. It isn't easy. Noteworthy performance requires resonance, breath control and exquisite change of pace; that is why it almost never works in print. Whether "dirty words" are lettered on a telephone booth with a felt-tip pen or set in a classic typeface in the newest best-seller, to me they always seem flat, lifeless and removed from human experience. Perhaps the problem with them in "girl talk" is that a soprano seldom gives them the punch they get from a robust baritone or bass. However, this also may be only the result of the conditioning of long years of habit.

There's an amusing episode starring Mark Twain, who in his day was almost as noted for his pyrotechnical profanity as for his narrative skill. Twain's new bride undertook to break his habit of swearing by memorizing all the objectionable words he used and reciting them to him in an unbroken string one morning at the breakfast table. The author listened to her recitation without blinking and at the end of it gravely replied, "My dear, you have the words all right. You just don't have the *tune!*"

At any rate, man's ear is often offended by female utterances that are not pure as Ivory soap. I personally regret the fact that yesterday's shockers are being de-used by overuse and misuse, although I have always cherished the Park Avenue matron who stepped off the curb in front of her elegant apartment house and said, "Oh, shit! I stepped in number two!" It is lamentable that the words have been bandied about by both sexes until it is no longer possible to express rage, outrage or passionate conviction in terms that command immediate attention.

Just how effective such spare usage of Anglo-Saxonisms can be is seen in the example of a young executive woman I know. Swearing in her offices is so commonplace that no one seems to notice. But her own speech is habitually pristine enough for afternoon tea at a nineteenth-century rectory until she really wants to be emphatic. Then she translates her thoughts into the language her associates appear to understand best. Coming from her, the words seem so fresh and unusual that everyone within earshot is galvanized into instant attention.

An interesting sidelight on the uses of pornography in male-female relationships occurred when the Brown University Club took up headquarters with the Women's National Republican Club in Manhattan. When it developed that men and women would have to share the plumbing, the facility commonly known as the powder room was wallpapered with a "unisex print"—that is, a stylized repeat of pandas which had been rendered as sexless. When I had lunch at the club with Republican friends, I was fascinated to see that various unknown graffiti artists in this citadel of conservatism had endowed the pandas with genitalia. I have no way of knowing the gender of those club members (or guests) who provided the artistry, but the genitalia were, in every case, male. Since some of the Brown men, notably the old grads, had been loudly opposed to the club's move, it was assumed that one of them had contributed the artwork as a token of his resentment. No one, however, was ever sure. It was pointed out that there were Republican women of an artistic bent who also opposed the merger—and some of the appendages were less than flattering.

The new freedoms, social and sexual, have brought

some never-before questions into business, and while there are no easy answers, both sexes can get more out of the interchange of capabilities by observing basic human consideration. Here are some thoughts on the subject for executive women:

1. *Don't stand back· on ceremony waiting for chivalry to rise from the ashes, but when it does, accept it politely, if not gratefully.* Responding to apparent courtesy with rudeness looks uncivilized, whatever the other person's intent may be.

2. *Feel free to invite a male client or business associate to join you for a meal or drinks, and when you do, be sure to catch the check.* Don't hesitate that split second it takes to make him feel he really should pay. And if he invited you, don't grab the check as if he can't afford it—especially if you know he can't. Even if he works for you at coolie wages, let him pay when he has asked you. His male ego probably needs it.

3. *Don't subject a male guest to cavalier treatment in a restaurant or anywhere else.* Maybe he's a traditionalist who isn't quite up on the new etiquette. What can you possibly gain by embarrassing the man? Does your own ego really need it?

4. *Watch your language.* (There may be gentlemen present!) Although movies, television, books and female people from eight to eighty have conditioned most ears to raunchy rhetoric, there's no point in offending anybody who prefers laundered language.

11

Fellow Travelers

Women who make frequent out-of-town business trips with men complain bitterly that it's an exhausting bore, a portal-to-portal ordeal requiring extra hours of extra-hard work plus constant attention to clothes, makeup, hair and all the details of business that the men either forget or refuse to be bothered with. Women who do not make these trips complain just as bitterly that it's day-in day-out drudgery, interrupted by nothing more fascinating than phone calls from the traveling playgirl who is probably languishing beside the pool, thinking up things for the slaves to do back at the office.

No one will ever convince the ones who are left behind that the traveler is really working. As for the woman orbiting the earth at company expense, she'll never admit that a minute of it was anything other than torture.

Somewhere between the two plaints lies a tenuous truth. The out-of-town trip can be fun, depending on where it is, who's with you and what you're expected to accomplish. A few other assorted blessings and curses do sometimes become part of the act such as dramatic extremes of weather and other acts of God, to say nothing of actions motivated by the devil himself.

These trips can be a waste of time and money, in addition to being physically grueling, but they can also be extremely valuable. They give you an opportunity to meet people who may have a key role in what you're trying to accomplish, and being on friendly terms with these people can help. When they set out to show and tell you the esoterica of their particular function in the business, no matter how much more you may know about it than they do, look and listen with respect. Most people take pride in their skills and enjoy having them appreciated. Even if what they're doing looks like a routine that could be taken over by a trained chimpanzee, try to pay attention and be properly impressed, but be careful not to go so overboard with your comments that your sincerity becomes questionable.

I have watched the processes involved in the manufacture of soap, cereal, automobiles, guitars, batteries, sausage, television sets, stereo equipment, hearing aids, cosmetics, beer, bourbon, bidets and a parade of other products. The most frightening spectacle I ever saw was the production of glass at an Owens-Corning Fiberglas plant near Providence, Rhode Island. Witnessing that required putting on protective goggles and peering into a blast furnace that was a vision of hell itself. The only process I ever refused to watch was ritual slaughter in a kosher meat-packing plant. One of the men in our group gratefully joined me in sitting that one out, and the man with the long knife was understanding. He said that some visitors faint—and he much preferred decliners to fainters.

On the assumption that you are not going to be subjected to something that will cause you to swoon dead away or throw up, it's unwise to avoid out-of-town trips to the factory or visits to customers in another city. Taking advantage of such opportunity indicates special interest in your job and the willingness to work beyond the nine-to-five schedule that is the prerogative of labor but seldom the practice of management. I have known women who became too "important" to leave the executive suite once they reached it. While it may seem appropriate to pass off this kind of detail to underlings, it's never smart for you to be less *au courant* with anything in the company than the people who report to you. So okay—

they do report. Let's assume they fill you in thoroughly on everything they see and hear. But let's also assume that you would have seen and heard something they didn't; if not, maybe you shoudln't be boss. Be sure your employees have an opportunity to learn all they can about the business, but at the same time be sure you know more about it than they do.

Now's the Time to Watch the Clock

Whether you're the boss already or a woman on the way, when you travel on company business you are, of course, very likely to be accompanied by male associates. Regardless of your rank, the first thing for any woman on the move with men to cultivate is breathtaking on-times-manship. Men may give everyone concerned a total nervous collapse by missing the plane altogether or by galloping up to the gate so late that all hands have lost hope. But under no circumstances (repeat, under no circumstances) may you or any other female arrive one second past the appointed time. Though hell should bar the door, in the best tradition of "the Highwayman," *be there on time*. The trouble is that even if you do have a punctuality record that would put NBC programming to shame, the cartoonists and comedians have established you as a member of the forever-tardy sex, a bumbling creature fidgeting with her hair rollers and talking on the telephone while the world whirls on, unheeded.

I had been working for a new company just six weeks when I was scheduled to make a trip to the Westinghouse plant in Mansfield, Ohio, with a group of four men. It was February, and the weather was so bad that all plane flights to the Midwest had been canceled. Even the birds were walking, so we made Pullman reservations on a train that left New York in the early evening and arrived in Mansfield early the next morning. When I went home to get ready for the trip, I unplugged an electric clock to plug in an iron and press a scarf. Preoccupied with packing, I forgot about the clock maneuver until I suddenly realized that the time had been 6:10 for much too long. I missed the train. Another railroad rattler was going in the same general direction an hour later, but it had no sleeping accommodations and was going no closer to Mansfield than Cleveland, thirty miles away. I took it, to find myself bumping morosely through the long night in an ancient railroad car that would have been too quaint for anybody except Walt Disney. No food or drink graced the train, and I had scrambled aboard so hurriedly that I didn't even have anything to read.

After struggling off the coach in Cleveland in a blinding snowstorm, I managed to persuade a cab driver that he should brave the ice and drifting snow to get me to Mansfield. He negotiated like a terrorist with hostages, but I paid up. Arriving at the meeting triumphantly—only twelve minutes late!—I expected a brisk round of applause but, of course, didn't get it. The greeting: "Where the hell were you all night? We were worried." I was thereafter referred to by the men in the group as "the late Miss Foxworth." When I got back home, I threw the electric clock in the trash and cluttered my apartment with all kinds of alarms and timing devices. I was never again late to a meeting with any of the group, but I never lived the episode down.

It isn't fair, but it *is* a fact. Men are strongly inclined to consider any woman who goes on a business trip with them excess baggage. That goes for you, too, even if you're a sweetheart in a million and at least one of the men on the trip is out of his mind about you. Getting out of town represents blessed escape for most men, and having you along kills some of that sensation of freedom. In fact, you may even be one of the things they're trying to escape. If you're the boss, the situation is different—on the minus side—because you can be sure you're high on the get-away-from list. Whatever the situation, though, the men will feel obliged to "look after" you or go through the motions anyway. So try to make it easy on everybody, especially yourself.

If you travel often or on sudden notice, keep a bag packed with all the basics. That way you won't be likely to wind up in some godforsaken motel without your make-up base and the only medication in the world that can stop your sneezing fits. There was a wondrous time when you could depend on the hotel and its drugstore to supply anything you might need. But no more. Chances are, you'll be staying in some little orange-and-green plastic fleabag where the nearest thing to a drugstore is a vending machine that swallows a handful of your quarters before you realize it's out of toothpaste, Bufferin and nail nippers.

Should you be the unfortunate kind of airplane passenger who takes off with wet palms and lands with wet pants, accept both my sympathy and absolute assurance that you'll get over it. If I could overcome the abject terror I used to feel in the air, anybody at all can—and after the first million miles up there I did. For at least ten years I was a chicken flier, deeply convinced that if God had intended us to fly, we would have been born with four or five ounces of straight gin in our veins. When Captain Mumbles got on the intercom with his cheery little bulletins, I was never reassured. It always occurred to me that if he couldn't fly any better than he could talk and if the engines weren't working better than the intercom system, we were in as much trouble as I had suspected since takeoff.

I am deliriously happy to say that I will now fly in anything that can get off the ground, and I frequently have to. Recently, I was in Oakland, Maryland, doing some work for a chain of stores located through West Virginia, Pennsylvania, Maryland and Ohio. Since the only way to visit a number of them quickly is via private plane, the chain's twenty-five-year-old advertising director, Mick Feld, owns and operates a Cessna Skyhawk II for that purpose. (Mick is an heir to the company and can afford it.) "Say, Jo," he said to me one morning, "why don't we take a look at a few stores today. Would you be afraid to fly with me?"

"Certainly not!" I replied, knowing him to be an international rowing champion and, therefore, a man of uncommonly fine reflexes. My enthusiasm died horribly when we were joined at the airport by a flight instructor, whose presence revealed the fact that Mick had only recently begun to take flying lessons. We spent the day practicing takeoffs and landings on small airstrips and pasture flats in the mountains of West Virginia—some of the least friendly terrain for emergency landings in the country. However, we also saw seven stores that day, and I was back in Pittsburgh in time to catch a six o'clock plane to New York.

Most advertising people have too much imagination to enjoy life in the air, so I have frequently been accompanied by men who were as nervous about flying as I was. One of them, "Alvin Ewing," was more so. Al had such dramatic anxiety attacks that the task of getting him onto the plane helped quell my own terrors. All my life I've heard of people "breaking out into a cold sweat," but he is the only person I ever saw do it. Perspiration would gush down the sides of an ashen face and flow off the tip of his nose, soaking his tie and shirt collar. At the call for boarding, Al's eyelids would start to flutter like the wings of a rabid bat, and he would be almost immobilized with fright. One or more of us would grasp his arms and propel him firmly into the aircraft. He would stumble to his seat as mournfully as a man headed for the electric chair and, after strapping himself in tightly enough to cut off circulation, would start demanding martinis. At six o'clock in the morning, as it sometimes was, that was hardly feasible, and when the stewardess refused, Al would announce that as soon as we reached ten thousand feet, he was going to throw her out of the plane. One early morning, when an unsympathetic stewardess was in no mood to shrug off his behavior, she threw *him* out of the plane before we left the gate—while every passenger within earshot cheered. I think he was actively sorry we didn't crash. In his mind it would have justified his terrified behavior.

Although I'm sure that I was every bit as terrified as Al, I didn't dare let it be known. To show it in any way or even admit it would have been to underline my gender and cause the men present to wonder whether I could really handle my part of the project under way. Al's reluctance to join the birds was dismissed as an amusing little eccentricity. Mine might easily have been recorded as a disqualifying weakness—yet another bit of proof that women have no business in business.

As time marched on, I became less afraid of flying because business responsibilities demanded that I do more and more of it. And as the responsibilities increased, so did my eagerness to rise above them. It's actually a wonderful feeling to be up there where nobody on earth can reach you—except via an emergency message from the pilot's cabin. (And it had better be a genuine emergency!) Just being at least thirty thousand feet away from the nearest telephone is, to me, worth the price of the flight.

"Ricky Richardson," who at twenty-seven is a sportswear merchandise manager for one of the big retail chains, makes frequent trips to the West Coast which she used to dread. But now she adores those hours on the plane when she doesn't have to quarrel on the phone for a single minute with store managers and suppliers. "Anyway," says Ricky, "after a dozen totally uneventful flights I finally got it through my head that it's true what they say about the safety of air travel: The most dangerous part of it is the trip to the airport."

Smile! You're on Trial

Aside from the flight itself, Murphy's Law works overtime on the out-of-town trip. Anything that can possibly go wrong usually does, and it's important (indeed, mandatory!) for you to be "a good sport" about it. The men may be bitching their brains out over lost luggage, loused-up reservations, the damned rented car, the weather, but the moment you join in on the chorus of complaint the higher pitch of your voice will cut your behavior out of the herd and label it as female. So no matter how heartily you despise your room, room service or anything else about the hotel or motel, don't tell anybody but the manager—and do that when nobody's listening. You don't have to throw your weight around on the road just to prove that you're running the show back at home base. If brute force becomes necessary, let the men use it.

While some hotel accommodations turn out to be little better than the bunkhouse at a run-down camp, others can be overwhelmingly grand. Beth Fielding, a young comer in the movie industry who grew up with "the new poor" in the radical 1960s, says that she was embarrassed by the splendors of the George V when her company was shooting a film in Paris. She moved to one of those colorful little hotels on the Left Bank where the starving painters stay, convinced that she'd be happier and more productive with "reality" than luxe. After two days she crept quietly back to the other side of the Seine, declaring the reality too real. "Only make-believe poverty has glamour," she said. "The genuine article isn't fun at all!"

It developed that one of Beth's problems was the antique French plumbing. "That hole-in-the-floor arrangement they have is okay for men. But what's a woman supposed to do?" she asked. And that's all there was! European plumbing has baffled many a new traveler. All of us have heard stories about Americans doing a bit of quick laundry in the bidet, but these are usually the mistakes of men. The bidet does look like a dandy place to wash socks, and who can blame them?

Business travel outside the United States requires stamina, fast reflexes and patience in just about equal parts—all prodigious. The heaviest testing I've faced for all three was in Japan, a land that is half dream, half nightmare. I went there as a guest of Shiseido, the Orient's primary maker of fragrances and cosmetics and the largest manufacturer of these products in the world, topping even Avon and Revlon in sales. The Shiseido factory was leveled during World War II by General Doolittle's "thirty seconds over Tokyo" raid, but was rebuilt and restored to past dominance by the Fukuhara family, whose progenitors had founded it.

Fun with the Sons of the Rising Sun

Nothing can prepare a newcomer for the impact of Tokyo. It is assault and battery on all five senses at once —a wild blast of noise, color and motion. As the Japanese say, "It is indescriptable!" At the time my company was the advertising agency for Shiseido Cosmetics America, Inc., and my assignment in Tokyo was to assist Shiseido's advertising department in the preparation of an ad for *Vogue* magazine (the American edition). That meant I was to stand by in an advisory capacity while my Japanese associates created and produced the ad in every detail.

I like and admire the Japanese. We get along well together because for one thing, their outlook and manners closely resemble those of the American South. With Southerners, everything is always "just fine." Maybe the roof is leaking and the kitchen's empty, maybe the whole family's drunk or sick or certifiably insane, but when anybody inquires, "Everything's just fine!" and so it is with the Japanese. They are unfailingly polite and pleasant and the bearers of good tidings. They can't bear to give you any bad news, and while there *is* a word for "no" in their language, I'm told that they never use it. Certainly they don't use it in English, and they almost always refuse to accept it when you do. You can state an incontrovertible fact to a Japanese, and if it isn't what he wants to hear, he will smile happily or laugh heartily and say, "I don't think so." This means that he expects you to work the problem out, although he is much too courteous to put it so bluntly. (Just like my old Mississippi granddaddy!)

I use the masculine pronoun here because in Japan women seldom enter into business matters. There's been a recent women's revolution there, too, but the *organized* effort folded last year, when its leader gave up and went back home. (Mrs. Misako Enoki had an agreement with her husband which required her to resume full-time housewifery gracefully if her efforts to mobilize the women of Japan in a drive for equality had not succeeded in a certain length of time. She lost.) A lot of women in Tokyo and Osaka have come out of their kimonos and are wearing American jeans. They work in offices and stores, but their level is about the same as that of New York women in the days of the suffragettes.

Knowing that a woman looks best to a Japanese man

with her forehead pressed firmly on the tatami, I approached my assignment with some of the feeling Daniel must have had when he entered the lion's den. And I was not reassured by my introduction to Tokyo. The noise, the smell, the motion converged in one screaming attack that left me wondering what vagary of chance had cast me into a Tokyo taxi hurtled toward eternity by a speeding driver, who kept taking both hands off the steering wheel to beat his breast and yell, "Kamikaze pilot!" But the fun and excitement were there! Ginza at night, with all the electronic signs playing games in calligraphy, is enough to make Broadway's theater district look blacked out, and by day traffic all over Tokyo is a Mickey Mouse riot run upside down and backward.

The Japanese are the most gracious hosts on earth. Seven Shiseido representatives met me at the airport, and two of them were assigned to me as official guides and interpreters. Mr. Ando and Mr. Hosogoee had been instructed by their Shiseido superiors to be sure that I was immersed in Japanese tradition and culture, and their mission was accomplished by taking me through at least thirty temples and gardens. Between sorties through the idyllic countryside, we worked on the ad. Ostensibly I was the project boss, but under the circumstances it would have been folly to take that position seriously. Most of the men spoke English, but they seldom spoke it to me, preferring to communicate with me through an interpreter—a standard Japanese tactic.

Each morning we met in the Shiseido conference room to select a model, and each morning my hosts produced pictures of the same girl. She was a Japanese model who had undergone the eyelid surgery in which the canthus fold was clipped to give her the round-eyed look that many contemporary Orientals seem to covet. (Even some of the Japanese baseball players have had this eyelid operation because they consider themselves television stars.) Convinced as I am that the Japanese beauties are the most gorgeous creatures on earth, I despise that round-eyed look. To me the girls with the "fixed" eyelids appear perpetually startled, so every time this batch of pictures hit the table with the same model staring at us, I complimented the men on their taste—but suggested that we consider models whose features were traditionally Oriental.

They would gravely discuss the matter in Japanese, and periodically Mr. Ando would interrupt to explain to me that they were talking about sundry topics concerning the relationship of the model to sales. I knew better. I knew they were really talking about the stupid broad from New York. Still, I hung in there, and eventually they would rise, bow to each other and to me, and Mr. Ando would say, "We meet again tomorrow on exact same subject." Next day, exact same thing would happen.

The Japanese know, for sure, that to an American time is money. They use the cliché themselves, but to them it's a perfectly hilarious joke. "Well, time is money," they say, and collapse in hysterical laughter, knowing that time isn't money at all—money is money, and much harder to come by than tomorrow, which dawns regardless.

All these conferences lasted precisely two hours and forty-five minutes, and after five days of them I agreed that the round-eyed girl was the only choice to make. They had won the round, as they were to win all the others, in a process I came to recognize as Operation Wear-Down. The Japanese simply wear you down with delay and repetition. So it went through every step of the ad. They wore me down on every issue, but I learned more from them than they did from me. It was several years before I was able to apply the most important lesson they taught me: patience—infinite, unalterable patience, the Oriental waiting game that can carry a point for you when nothing else can.

It took three weeks to do an ad that could have been done in New York in three days—but New York has been at it a couple of generations longer. The Japanese businessmen can no longer be dismissed as "monkey-see, monkey-do imitators who never have an original idea" or "little men making little things." They are superb creators with dazzlingly original marketing ideas for products as large as steamships. And when they finally do admit their women to the upper levels of business (Mrs. Enoki notwithstanding), they will undoubtedly give us Westerners a hotter run for our money than we're getting now.

Mr. Ando and Mr. Hosogoee showed me how to eat rice with chopsticks on a train speeding along at 140 miles an hour, how to get onto a Tokyo subway so crowded that special pushers packed us in, how to keep cool in an automobile with one of those terry cloths wrapped in ice, and how to eat raw fish without flinching. They were great fellow travelers!

Whether you're headed for Tokyo or some remote hamlet in Michigan, out-of-town trips with men can be made happier and more productive if you try to remember these things:

1. *Be on time—regardless!* As a member of the sex that comedians have cast in a role of eternal tardiness, you can't afford to be late. Ever. As a woman you're expected to be late, but as an executive you're expected to be on time.

2. Fear of Flying *is a novel, not an acceptable trait for people who want to go places fast.* The world is full of "white-knuckle fliers" of both sexes, but if you intend to get very far in business, it's better not to advertise your own reticence to take to the air.

3. *Do not carp or carry on about your hotel ac-*

commodations, no matter how regrettable or splendid they may be. Seasoned travelers take such things in stride and save their breath for more important matters.

4. *Be a "good sport" about all the mishaps and inconveniences that sometimes plague a trip.* You've still got a job to do, so calm down and do it.

5. *Do not be dismayed when your associates in another country conduct business in their own language and by their own rules.* You can return the compliment when they're in your offices!

6. *In foreign countries remember that the foreigner is you.* Try to follow the local customs, and learn a few phrases of the local language. Even if you botch your pronunciation atrociously, your hosts and hostesses will be pleased that you care enough to try.

7. *As the cliché goes, stay loose.* Accept all the consequences of Murphy's Law (anything that can go wrong *will*) with equanimity, if not aplomb. You'll be marked so clearly as a sophisticated traveler that you'll never feel like an eggy-faced tourist again.

12

Drinking Things Over

Drinking things over is an ancient and honorabl business custom—grand for celebrating, commiserating introducing a new person or project, firing a friend o appeasing somebody whose blue suede shoes you'v stepped on. It's also an ancient and not-so-honorabl weapon, potentially as damaging as a blow on the hea with a bung starter.

Now that women are moving into the executive suit and picking up all the pressures of so-called men's job they are also picking up the privilege of "men's diseases —such stress-related ailments as bleeding ulcers, execu tive depression, early heart attacks, "male" vascular dis eases. And alcoholism.

Nobody knows how many alcoholics there are amon today's Boss Ladies because they are, understandably, re luctant to stand up for a nose count. But authorities agre that the number is rapidly rising, perhaps faster tha among suburban matrons, who increasingly are afflicte with what is known as the housewife's secret disease. An Boss Lady who bellies up to the bar with the boys—sits down with her male associates in a quiet cockta lounge—and proceeds to go at it with them on a drin for-drink basis is entering rugged terrain. Even thoug she may be a seasoned drinker who can "hold" her li uor, the odds are against her in almost any booze-o with the fellows—especially if it's not as friendly as sl has been led to believe.

While much remains to be learned about the effec of alcohol, intoxication appears to be a highly person matter. The amount of alcohol required to produce a state of euphoria, exhilaration or plain drunkenness varies from individual to individual. This is one of the few points on which the drinkers, bartenders and scientists have reached agreement. Of course, all dedicated drinkers consider themselves more reliable authorities on bacchanalia than any test-tube pusher. And bartenders are the self-declared keepers of all the earth's wisdom. (They got it talking to drunks!) But according to alcohol research chemists, size—or body weight—is the most significant single factor in determining the number of drinks a person can handle. Thus, a 130-pound woman drinking with a 180-pound man is at a 50-pound disadvantage from the start, much as a boxer would be facing an opponent who outweighs him by 50 pounds. Few boxers (a group not renowned for mental giantism) would put themselves in that kind of spot. Yet executive women whose intellect approaches genius happily plunge into drinking bouts that find them as ill-matched.

Cheers, girls! And here's luck! You're going to need it.

Some women can drink some men all the way under the table, some of the time. But it goes the other way more often. And a man under the table can still be dangerous—if not tonight, tomorrow. Even though he simply lapses into unconsciousness and lies quietly on the carpet, disturbing no one and nothing, you can be certain he'll hate himself in the morning. You can also be certain that admiration will be the last emotion he'll feel for the girl who outdrank him.

If you can do it, don't. Quit while he's ahead. If you're blessed with a "hollow leg," celebrate your God-given talent only with men who love you enough to forgive and forget. But most men in your offices won't. Drink one of them senseless, and long after his self-esteem has struggled back to normal, he'll be more sheepish than

happy any time he sees you. About the only way he ca
get even is to drop a few well-placed hints that you're
real, live lush—and don't think he won't do it!

Of course, if the face on the barroom floor is you
own, it's *Götterdämmerung* for sure. The best way t
circumvent either possibility is to avoid any big drink-up
with business associates or cut them short by advanc
planning. Better you should miss out than mess up. Th
warm, hearty camaraderie isn't worth it.

Here's to a Few Quick Ones—and Here's How!

Drinking with male business associates requires in
finite tact and caution. A young woman in publishing ha
told me about some of the problems she has had drinkin
with authors. She has built-in power because the write
whose work is published by her company depend on he
for advice and guidance that can be translated into in
come. Providentially she's one of those apparent inno
cents with a hollow leg, an enormously handy appendag
in her line of work. "I don't know whether writers are ac
tually thirstier than other people," she says. "But the one
who want to take me out drinking certainly seem to b
Of course, they're terribly tense about their work—wri
ers' nerves—and this causes liquor to hit them harder. N
matter. They want to keep pub crawling, especially
they don't live in New York. And they want to show m
the city (as if I hadn't seen it before!), plying me wit
drinks as a gesture of appreciation and, as the evenin
wears on, affection.

"It's really rather sweet," she continues. "A wonde
ful way to get to know a writer rather quickly. But it ca
be wearing, too. I don't dare relax and wander over th
tipsy line, because if I did, this would give him an excus
to become 'protective'—that is, possessive—the galla

male guardian taking care of 'his' editor. The power I hold in our relationship would pass over to him right then and there, and I'd never get it back!"

Another woman, who is marketing director for a large cosmetics company, tells me that she has drinking problems with men who manage various product groups in her department. "Sometimes there aren't enough hours in the day to take care of all the details," she says. "So at six or seven o'clock in the evening I go out with one of the managers I'm working with. Most of them are reasonable. But one or two try to press several lethal drinks on me too fast. This may be done out of a well-meant desire to please me. But I can't help wondering if the man's motivation may be a little wish to 'get something on me.' At any rate, I don't like it and always feel that the situation creates unnecessary tension between us."

Although my home state was the last bastion of Prohibition in the Union, drinking was a game that anyone there with a low boredom threshold got into early. There wasn't much else to do. Until 1963 an article of the constitution of Mississippi prohibited the sale, purchase, possession or consumption of any alcoholic beverages other than 3.2 percent beer, which became legal in some counties after repeal of the Volstead Act. But an amendment to that article levied a 10 percent sales tax on all alcoholic beverages sold in the state, hard liquor and wine included. Strange as it may seem to outsiders, this kind of legal ambivalence was perfectly understood by Mississippians and largely approved. The state got extra revenue, the drinking people got their liquor and the Baptist Church could still proudly point out that Mississippi was dry. Only the bootleggers were unhappy. The tax was a bother to them, and immediately after it was levied in 1942, they damned it as the Black Market Tax.

It was in the midst of this weird, almost schizophrenic attitude toward alcohol that I did my first "business drinking." Since bars and cocktail lounges were against the law, it was necessary to obtain booze by the bottle, and the whole bottle was usually consumed at one sitting as a matter of course. With drinking illegal, the game was to destroy the evidence as quickly as possible, and drinking it seemed the best way. Getting a bottle of anything at all was never a problem in Mississippi except when political expediency dictated a crackdown on the bootleggers who flourished all through the state. In the river and coast towns well-publicized liquor stores operated openly—in some cases around the clock, even on Sundays and holidays. Elsewhere in the state equally well-publicized sellers operated out of hotel pantries, shacks in the woods, taxicab fleets and suburban family garages (whose owners shared the profits). Some restaurants and nightclubs in counties that had cooperative law enforcement officers sold bottles to trusted patrons, and most displayed small, tasteful tent cards on the table reading: "Out of respect for our local authorities, please keep your bottle bagged and under the table."

I first became aware of liquor as weaponry in the Jackson, Mississippi, department store where my career began. In addition to working an intimate part of my anatomy off making newspaper layouts and writing copy, I made the crucial decisions about what was to be advertised—and where. This gave me a certain amount of clout with the various buyers, who wanted their merchandise pushed, and with the media reps (advertising salesmen), who understandably wanted it pushed via the broadcast time and newspaper space they were selling.

I was born either thirsty or two drinks behind everybody else. Additionally, I am easily depressed by small things, like seven o'clock in the morning. In any event, I have always felt warmly cheered up by a couple of drinks, and this propensity of mine quickly became known in an area where liquor had the added glamour of illegality, to say nothing of the sinful connotation placed on it by the Baptist Church. Since the sons of the store owner I worked for were, respectively, an alcoholic and a teetotaler, the situation was decidely delicate. Nobody knew how the patriarch felt about the polarity of his sons' drinking habits, but it wasn't considered a good idea to test him—about that or anything else. Consequently, any thirst quenching done was done secretly, which naturally made it more fun.

In those days I drank with a great deal more enthusiasm than wisdom and got myself into some situations that were embarrassing and untenable, to say the least. Drinking with anybody at that time was correctly called splitting a jug, and I learned the hard way that if I split a jug with an advertising salesman or a buyer, I was expected to grant him special favors in the dispensation of newspaper space or broadcast time. Some of my bottled-in-bond companions were crafty enough to insist later that I had made grand-scale promises to them at the bottom of the jug; this gave me an uncomfortable sense of being somehow in their debt, if not actually in their power.

Although there were at least half a dozen alcoholics in key executive spots at the store where I worked, only one of them was fired for drinking. You guessed it—a Boss Lady. This was a buyer whose problem came to the attention of management when she fell and broke a leg after splitting a jug with a salesman who didn't feel constrained to see her home from their revels. I hope he never got another order from anybody. I know he never got another one from her in the bigger, better job she landed after drying out—and he actually had the temerity to complain about it.

Time Does Change Everything—Even Madison Avenue and Booze

In New York and all over the country, the advertising business is still trying to live down the hard-drinking, hell-raising reputation it picked up two whole generations ago, when, if one believes the stories, it really was more fun and games than business. Today the field has become so hotly competitive that few people in it can afford the luxury of a day-to-day hangover, and the three-hour, four-drink lunches that used to be SOP are now the mark of the neophyte, the amateur dabbler or the unemployed.

When I first went to work on Madison Avenue, a few dedicated drinkers were still around. One of these, Kev Sledge, was a bourbon man who carried a bottle with him for emergencies. One recurring emergency was the Westinghouse plant in Mansfield, Ohio, where he frequently had to journey to visit a valued client. The plant was an emergency because there were no drinking facilities in or near it, so Kev took the special precaution on these trips of slipping a small bottle into his pocket. At one memorable meeting he arose to explain the storyboard for a television commercial and the unmistakable stench of cheap bourbon arose with him. In lurching to his feet, he had struck the bottle at just the right or wrong angle, causing it to break and drench his pants with liquor. Kev gamely kept explaining the storyboard as the bourbon stain spread until the client finally said, "For Christ's sake, Kev, do you even *piss* booze?" Needless to say, if one of the Boss Ladies had broken a bottle of bourbon in her purse, neither the client nor the agency would have thought it forgivable—let alone funny.

Kathy Russell, the most dazzling ad writer I ever

knew, was another dedicated tippler who was delightfully ingenious at ordering a huge belt of straight gin. She did it with her special copywriter's flair every time she ordered a martini. "Waiter," she would say, "please listen very carefully. I want an icy cold, crystally clear, very, very, *very* dry, very, *very* dry martini." Then, as he turned away, she would sing out, "Oh, waiter, please— no vermouth at all. And make that a double!"

Kathy has gone on to greater glories, writing successful books and articles in another city. She got out just in time. I'm sure that if she had stuck around, she'd be miserable with the drinking habits that prevail in the ad business today. Martinis are known as Instant Idiocy or Silver Loudmouths, and almost nobody ever drinks them anymore. Light drinks are in: tall scotches with soda, daiquiris (still popular after having been made acceptable by JFK), and in warm weather gin and tonic, vodka and tonic or spritzers (white wine with soda). White wine is growing in popularity as a year-round tipple, and at cocktail parties there is an increasing run on the chablis. And there is a surge of interest in Perrier water among people who prefer no alcohol at all.

Most women who drink—whether a lot or a little— appear to enjoy it as much as their male companions do, but until recently not many of us were willing to admit a genuine liking for the stuff. Even businesswomen would insist they drink only to be sociable, to keep the men from feeling self-conscious or to avoid seeming out of place. While all this is undoubtedly true, one suspects that it is not the whole truth and nothing else but. Executive women, as well as men, like the sense of release and relaxation induced by a bit of alcohol, plus the feeling of confidence and importance that warms them after a few drinks. Their emotional need for these sensations is at least as deep as that of men, and in business situations the need is likely to be even deeper. For businesswomen need all the courage and sense of worth they can get, and some of them are slow to realize the kind that's poured out of a bottle is deceptive only to themselves.

Happily, however, the career woman who has become overinvolved with alcohol is more apt to get help at an early stage than her male business associates or even housewives, simply because she'll be forced to by the old heave-ho. While the male alcoholic is often "protected" by co-workers and even management, the lady lush—like that buyer I worked with in Jackson, Mississippi—almost always gets a swift and succinct adieu rather than admission to the company's alcohol program. The same jolly good fellows who close ranks around one of their own who feels too jolly too often, will set new speed records mustering a bibulous Boss Lady out of the corps. Similarly, a husband who will tolerate and hide the condition of his alcoholic wife indefinitely will summarily dismiss a woman in his employ the moment he discovers she has a drinking problem. While he may feel bound by vow, by duty and by fear of embarrassment to live with the situation at home, he's not about to put up with a boozing dame at the office.

This is probably all to the good for the boozing career girl. Getting fired can provide the jolt she needs to accept her drinking problem as a serious illness—even if it's not nearly so far advanced as that of the man in the office next door who just got a promotion in spite of the daily bottle in his desk drawer.

Actually this double standard is observed as rigidly by women as it is by men. The girls will forgive the guys their alcoholic trespasses with ease and grace—but not each other's. The two-fisted male drinker often maintains an image of reckless decadence that is all but irresistible to women. He is the *bon vivant,* the romantic rogue, the wild man-on-the-town whose drinking may be associated with adventure, hedonism, even virility. But the hard-drinking executive woman is solidly denounced by the very girls who admire and adore her sauced-up male associates without reservation. And men in or out of business seldom equate her tippling with sexiness or find themselves overcome by desire for her when she's drinking with abandon.

Who Says I'm Bombed?

Our attitudes, male and female, are strongly conflicted about drinking. Women, who account for a fair share of the 300 million gallons of alcohol consumed by Americans annually, might be interested in some ground rules set up by Dr. Leon A. Greenberg, Yale University's internationally known authority on the anatomy of intoxication. Dr. Greenberg prepared the following information in the 1960s and to my knowledge no subsequent developments have superseded it.

Dr. Greenberg established that an adult whose weight is 150 pounds can drink one whiskey highball or six ounces of table wine or three and one-half ounces of sherry or two bottles (regular size) of 4.5 percent beer with little change in feeling or functioning. Assuming that the individual has had no dinner and has downed any of the above-named "cheers" within a short span of time, Dr. Greenberg calculated that the content of alcohol in the drinker's bloodstream soon reaches .03 percent.

A second round, hard on the heels of the first, doubles that percentage to .06, the point at which one begins to feel a glow. Here's where you might start table-hopping to greet minor acquaintances or strike up a conversation with a stranger. Round three, following swiftly, sends the count up to .09 percent, producing exaggerated or perhaps emotional behavior—such as assuring the boss or a client that he's the greatest thing since the aerosol bug bomb. The fourth drink raises the level to .12 percent, causing some impairment of "fine coordination" and slight-to-moderate unsteadiness. Here the drinker might give in to a long-harbored yearning to inform the boss or client that he isn't greater than the bug bomb at all, but really king of the jerks, unworthy of the talent around him that he so ruthlessly exploits.

The fifth one does it! Here the blood alcohol content climbs to .15 percent, and that's intoxication, legally and otherwise—"unmistakable abnormality in gross bodily functions and mental faculties." What happens after this point of alcoholic pollution is reached in the blood becomes a highly personal ball game. The drinker may fall down, throw up or pass out; laugh or cry or sing; do any or all of these things or maybe just wander around "on instruments" like a plane approaching a socked-in airport. An aging ad man I knew—one whose drinking habits dated back to Madison Avenue's carefree era— once brought a pigeon back from lunch and released it in the McCann-Erickson boardroom during a crucial meeting.

Dr. Greenberg's computations are, of course, rejected by most barroom quarterbacks, who have an endless supply of legends about jockeys, midgets and eighty-pound girls who could drink the biggest of the brand blasters senseless and march bravely into the dawn without a bobble. Some of them may even be true. Of course, there *are* factors other than body weight in Dr. Greenberg's equations that affect the drinking capacity of any given person at any given time. These include hunger, fatigue, general health, the emotional state of the drinker and the period of time over which the drinks are consumed. It takes two hours for each drink to disappear from the bloodstream of a 150-pound body, so that's four hours for two drinks, six hours for three and so on. Accordingly, if the 150-pound drinker were to stretch five drinks over a period of ten hours, he would probably never get beyond the buzz state. But how many people do you know who drink like that? And how many women remember that when they weigh less, they need more time between drinks.

Moreover, all individuals do have their own particular tolerance for alcohol, which Leon D. Adams, a longtime researcher in the alcoholic beverage field and one of the founders of the Wine Institute, christened the "A.Q." (alcohol quotient). Mr. Adams points out that this is a "highly individualized statistic." In *The Commonsense Book of Drinking,* he advises that if you drink at all, you should learn the number of drinks of what kind, what size and what power you can handle under a given set of conditions. That sounds like a life's work. And to make matters more complicated, Adams warns, "Experiment with caution, lest you learn the hard way that your 'A.Q.' is lower than average."

Drinking is a wobbly crutch when used to overcome shyness or to brace oneself for a big appearance or performance. The career woman who steadies herself with a pair of stiff drinks before making a luncheon or dinner speech won't necessarily become a desk-drawer drinker, but she's a lot more likely to wander into the habit of tossing off a few before any important presentation or meeting than the Boss Lady who walks into the baby-pink spotlight steadied only by thorough preparation and rehearsal.

I once worked with a woman who suffered anguishing anxiety attacks before client presentations—that is, meetings at which new advertising programs were shown for the first time to client organizations. Things were okay if the meetings were held after lunch, but she was once assigned an account whose client group insisted that the meetings be held at 8:45 A.M. sharp. "Inhuman!" Jill screamed. "I can't face a critical audience—I can't face any audience—without a few drinks!" What happened was that she would set the clock for 6 A.M., get up and have coffee first, then two ounces of vodka and orange juice. She'd rehearse her presentation until 6:30, then eat a twelve-ounce steak, have another vodka, shower and dress. At 8:30 she'd be at the office, where she'd hit herself in the face with yet another vodka before going in to make the presentation. She always performed brilliantly, and when her triumphant meeting ended, she flew into a relieved celebration. But the routine did finally get to her, and Jill today is a 220-pound alcoholic.

One of the smartest women I know—merchandise manager for one of New York's big retail operations—says that she'd rather drink than do anything else but almost never does, for the very reason that she likes it too much. "Besides," she says, "it's just plain dumb to drink with business associates, and when I socialize at all, it's usually with some of them. I used to get into some pretty spirited drink-it-ups with the other bosses. But I found out that men who praised my talents extravagantly when we were out on the town would hunt hard for holes in my work the next day. The degree of their criticism would correspond directly to the number of drinks I'd had, and this would go on not just the next day but for days afterward. I'd have to pitch in and prove all over again that I really was interested in my job and not just another lady lush."

Unfortunately that's the way it goes. You particularly can't expect sympathy if you stumble in late, looking hung-over and feeling as if you'd been run over by a garbage truck. Your best bet after a night of riotous living is to bound out of bed thirty minutes early no matter how much it hurts and soak for twenty-five minutes in a warm bath. It's the equivalent of four hours' sleep and a lovely relaxant for muscles and nerves, as well as a tremendous lift for the psyche. Eat a field hand's breakfast, paint yourself a convincing false face, put on your best-looking clothes and arrive at the office smack on the dot —it it kills you. Do not wear dark glasses, a sure sign of indiscretion. But if your eyes really do look like two fried eggs in clabber or pee holes in the snow, it's better to put on dark glasses anyway and complain that you were hit in the eye by a piece of flying trash.

Nowadays I drink almost nothing, but I feel free to dispense advice with the same heavy hand I've always used when pouring drinks. Here are a few handy tips for tipplers to take or leave alone:

1. *Know your own A.Q., and if you don't like it, try to respect it.* Remember that your alcohol quotient is a highly personal thing, like a whistle space between the teeth or the sixth finger that one of Henry VIII's wives had on each hand. Your A.Q. may not be related to that of your drinking companion or to Dr. Greenberg's guidelines. Most of the accomplished drinkers I've talked to about the Greenberg drunk table tend to write it off as science fiction. They blithely announce that they could handle five drinks when they were in the third grade— during the 20-minute recess. Maybe so. But you may be one of the unfortunates who can't get past two without going into the giggles, weeps, hiccups or something even less attractive.

At any rate, you can find your range through cautious experiment. And once you've found it, don't push it unless you really want to get smashed. Even if you don't keep track of the number of drinks you down, your trusty corpuscles will. They'll be in there computing your blood alcohol content as ruthlessly as any IBM machine, and when it hits .15 percent, you've had it, legally, physically and socially, no matter how many or how few drinks it took to get there.

2. *If it looks like a long, hard party, pick a light*

drink and stick to it. And be advised, if you aren't already, that sherry is not one of them. Where I was born and raised, many a sweet little old lady has wound up in the oleander bushes or has been piggybacked upstairs with an attack of the vapors because she thought sherry was only a little stronger than orange Nehi. Sherry is a fortified wine, which means that the kick has been boosted by the addition of more alcohol to that produced naturally by ferment, and three and a half ounces of it pack the same wallop as the average bartender's highball, Manhattan or whiskey sour.

Travel abroad has brought popularity to wine of all kinds, and most of the unfortified ones deliver only half the punch of a regular highball or cocktail. It's socially acceptable to sip wine all evening if you want to, and you may even mix it with soda. Of course, you can get out of your mind on wine if you drink it fast enough. The winos do all the time. But sipped conservatively, it can coast you through a rough evening without landing you in the oleander bushes or upstairs in a strange bed.

3. *If you don't drink, don't apologize.* When you don't want another cheer or don't even want the first one, "No, thank you" will do. Trying to explain is both pointless and asinine. Most people really don't care whether you drink or not as long as you don't interfere with their own wishes in the matter. Here and there you may make somebody self-conscious, and if you'd rather not risk this, you may prefer to make a joke of it, but as the Boss Lady you're as free to decline as you are to invite the others to go ahead.

4. *If you're just a girl who can't say no, eat and cheat.* So you're the convivial type, the orally compulsive kind of Boss Lady who enjoys being talky and witty and charming—and you automatically reach for another glass every time the drink tray goes by. Before the festivities start, eat something—bits of meat, cheese, eggs, any good

protein in sufficient quantity to give you a substantial base for drinking. Also, you might try the European trick of swallowing a couple of tablespoons full of olive oil or cream before the party. The Scandinavians, who are notorious "hollow leggers," gulp charcoal pills before flying into the aquavit, on the theory that these have some magic power to "absorb" alcohol. One thing is sure: Eating does slow down the progress of alcohol into the blood, and if you keep drinking, you should keep eating—and worry about getting fat tomorrow.

But if you're seriously dieting, don't drink at all. Or do limit your alcoholic intake according to the limit you've placed on calories. That famous dieting cry "Calories Don't Count" is another wishful myth. Calories, liquid or solid, do count. And if you're limiting the solids, be sure to limit the liquids, too.

5. *If you catch a hangover, tough it out.* There are only two cures for this affliction—twenty-four hours or death. Everybody who drinks with any degree of enthusiasm or regularity will, sooner or later and usually sooner, wake up with the indescribable disease known, for want of a better name, as a hangover. The ailment has as many exquisite variations as the drinks that produce it. If you were to experience the same symptoms against any other background of recent behavior, your first thought would be to call an ambulance and demand to be sped to the nearest hospital emergency ward. But since it's "just a hangover," the only thing to do is whatever you were supposed to do that day.

Expect no sympathy, for (as indicated earlier in this chapter) you won't get it, even from your drinking partners of the night before. If they feel as bad physically as you do, you can be sure they feel as rotten emotionally, too. Alcohol, after all, isn't really a stimulant. It's a depressant, a bleak fact that becomes painfully clear the next day.

The late Eddie Condon's famous remedy for a hangover ("Take the juice of two quarts of whiskey . . .") is only for people who are prepared to devote their lives to acquiring and curing hangovers on a full-time basis. The best thing to do is rise above it. As they say in the Navy, answer the bell. Get up and get cracking. Eat, no matter how unpleasant the thought of food may be. Avoid the hair of the dog, and above all, don't admit you have a hangover. You'll probably feel that everybody you meet knows what an aching, shaking wreck you are inside, but don't tell a soul. Keep your misery to yourself, and as a friend of mind at the *New York Times* says, prove that a dead snake can twitch till sundown.

13

The Inquisition

Every company has its "curiosity index," and nothing pops it to the top faster than a new person on the premises. The whole tribe becomes a personal research organization dedicated to collecting the newcomer's vital statistics at once. The statistics that are most vital are age, sex habits and salary, and there are always people around who will stop at nothing to *find out*. If the new arrival is a man, the approach is unfailingly wary, but when it's a woman, that's a caveat of a different color. People feel free to ask women those sensitive little questions they would hesitate to ask men. The lines of interrogation used to extract the information may be subtle and circumlocutious or disarmingly direct, but clever women won't trip over either trap.

"Sylvia Grant," a brand manager I know who is rising fast in the cigarette business, told me about a man in her company who invited her to lunch the first week she was there and, even before the Bloody Marys landed on their table, opened up like this: "I know you have to be older than you look to have such an important job—and I'm very interested in you. How old *are* you, Sylvia, dear?"

Boom! Just like that. Direct question, right there on the restaurant table.

Sylvia flashed him her finest smile and said, "My grandfather was *so* amusing. He always said that a woman tells her age and a man tells his income only to lie about it! Let's keep our conversation pure! Tell me about your department."

No fool, that Sylvia. First of all, *she* didn't put her interrogator down—she quoted her grandfather and let him do it. Hearing dear old Gramp's amusing observation, Sylvia's interrogator had to assume that if she told him her age, then he might be expected to tell her his salary—and she wouldn't believe any figure he came up with anyway. By the same token, neither could he be sure about the age she gave him! The poor man was happy to change the subject to his department.

Sometimes a direct question like that (surprise attack!) is so disarming that a woman, tipped off-balance, will blurt out the answer. But that's never a wise move, even if you're very young and extremely proud to be so far advanced at such a tender age. Astute game players know endless ways to turn youth into a drawback as hobbling as retirement age. Ten years from now it will be another story anyway, and the statistics will have found their way into the public domain.

Here are some other lighthearted replies I've heard that sidestep the question:

"Oh, my, let's not count each other's teeth. I'm still too excited by the company to think about myself. Tell me what's happening in your department."

"Did you read that wonderfully wicked thing in *Esquire* from Truman Capote's new book? A man at a cocktail party was wondering out loud about the age of a girl there, and his wife said, 'For heaven's sake, George, why don't you chop off her legs and count the rings!' No chopping, today—please! I'd much rather hear what you're doing about thus-and-so in your department."

Answers like this not only get you off the hook but bring the subject back to business. Your questioner may be disappointed not to have learned your age, but he can hardly afford to quarrel with your interest in the company and his specific area of responsibility there.

The "subtle" or circumlocutious lead-in must be dealt with in kind and requires continuing vigilance. In this method the inquisitor seeks to "date" you by association—with graduating classes, wars, elections, assassinations, anything that can link you to a particular time, person or event that could serve as an age indicator. "Sally Hunter" supplied the following dialogues from her experience at NBC:

Example:

Q. "I hear you went to Smith. I had a cousin there. Kim Middlebush. Wonder if you knew her? Class of '67 or thereabouts?"

A. "I'm afraid I was in a class by myself at Smith. I was on a real reading binge—a very serious student. Spent so much time buried in books I didn't get to know some of the people I should have. Getting ready to tackle this job."

Example:

Q. "I'll never forget the day Kennedy was shot, will you? Where were you when it happened?"

A. "I was at the movies. I'm the world's champion movie buff!"

Q. "You mean you weren't in school?"

A. "Nothing could come between me and the movies back then. Now my grand passion is my job!"

Marital status often gets a brisk workout ahead of age. Absolutely everybody feels free to ask if you're married—and woe to the woman who's not. Fielding questions about why not becomes so tiresome that many a woman takes refuge in a marriage that is meaningless or downright miserable. Unless you have two heads on a Quasimodo torso, it's easier than explaining. If you're reasonably attractive and unmarried at the moment, the investigating committee really bears down. You're a divorcée—poor dear, what happened? And what are you doing for sex these days? You're single—a nice girl like you, how come? Foolin' around with a married man? Ah! Wow! A lez!

Pinning down your sex life is assumed to be a simple matter, and the "ingenious" questions are entirely predictable. Marianne X, a fortyish knockout who has never married anybody and swears she never will, reports these exchanges with the private eyes at her firm:

Q. "You live alone, Marianne?"

A. "Remember Jack Nicholson's marvelous line in that movie when a woman phoned and asked, 'Are you alone?' He said, 'Isn't everybody?' Don't you think Nicholson's super?"

(The conversation's off to the movies.)

Q. You must live alone, Marianne—right?"

A. "Who's alone in a city of ten million people? I've been reading about the incredible increase in world population and. . . ."

(Who wants to talk about *that?* The questioner hurries away, changes the subject or takes off on it if the population disaster happens to be a favorite of his or hers.)

Q. "Aren't you afraid to live alone, Marianne?"

A. "I don't think I'd ever be afraid of anything. My grandfather used to quote from a poem. . . ."

(Ditto. Almost nobody wants to hear your old granddaddy's poetry quote, and the ones who do are buffs who'll want to lob a few lines back from their own beloved poetic repertoires.)

Q. "You have an apartment in the city, Marianne—by yourself?"

A. (Cheerfully distressed) "Apartments! Houses! Any mention of them reminds me of some decorating I want to do. Such a chore! But I saw an article in *House & Garden* that set me on fire. What do you think of a monochromatic color scheme? I want to do a living room in about five shades of blue. . . ."

In an era that runs toward revelation, even married women are hit by sex questions that it isn't smart to answer. Carol Burnett was recently subjected to one of those on a talk show (where innuendo and "frank" sex discussions are apparently highly prized). Helen Gurley Brown, who has made a career of the sex revolution, asked Miss Burnett outright, "Did you and Joe sleep together before you were married?"

Burnett's cool, level reply: "You know, somebody asked me that one time and I said it was none of their business."

Glorious! Of course, you can't indulge the luxury of an outright put-down as freely as Miss Burnett, but nobody has to answer questions like that. You can always just smile and leave your interrogator impaled on the tasteless question. It takes poise and guts—both qualities which any woman in business should develop.

Although salary information in most companies is supposed to be confidential, it miraculously finds its way into the public domain almost immediately. Rumors about what is being paid to whom are exchanged the way children trade gum, and the juicy fruit about your paycheck will probably be corridor talk even before you draw your first one.

All that the fact finders need from you is confirmation. Don't let them have it. They'll wheedle, goad, pry, trick, break out every tack short of truth serum and the rack itself, but don't endorse or deny anything. As long as you remain noncommittal, the rumors remain only that—rumors.

A favorite ploy is to burn you up with a piece of news, accurate or not, about what somebody else is getting for the same job as yours or one similar. Like: "Crockett made sixty thou a year when he had your department. Too bad this company won't pay that kind of money to a woman. I'm sure you do a better job." This is your cue to turn bright purple and make choking noises because you're only getting half that—or to flush with pride and inform your tormentor that you're being paid exactly the same amount, if not more. Wrong! Smile benignly. And say something terribly polite but vague about Crockett. If he really was getting more than you are, discussing it with the company CIA won't help your cause a bit.

Another example: "Do you know what a favor you did Miriam Belsen? She got a five-thousand-dollar raise when you came here. Wow! Forty-two thousand five hundred dollars! That means she's still the highest paid woman in the company, doesn't it?" Again, you're supposed to react as if you'd just been set upon by the Boston strangler or else lick the yellow feathers off your lips and admit that the highest paid woman in the company is little you. Don't. Just say you don't know Miriam very well but hope to get better acquainted because she strikes you as being a very able person.

And another: "You hear what happened to Francine? The company's giving her a condo in Westport as a bonus. I can't wait to hear what you're getting!" This pronouncement is expected to make you faint dead away or blab what everyone's waiting to hear about your bonus. Never! Remark unflinchingly on what a nice thing that is for Francine—she *enjoys* Westport!

If one of the rasher souls is brave enough to ask you a baldfaced question about your paycheck, perks or bonus, you can always dig up your old granddad and recycle his quote about lying on the subject of age and salary. Do it! It's fun.

In the immortal words of Casey Stengel, you don't have to tell nobody nuttin'. Practice smiling. And remember that an unanswered question is stickier for the asker than the askee. Keep the following points in mind:

1. *Don't tell your age to anybody*. You may be so proud of being the youngest executive in the history of the company that you'll be tempted to shout it from the air-conditioning tower, but you'll be another middle-aged executive someday and maybe not so eager to broadcast it.

2. *Don't tell your salary to anybody*. This is privileged information, and spreading it around can cause trouble to top management. Top managements hate trouble, and one of the first things you learn when you're running a company is why they're such bastards up there.

3. *Don't tell the fascinating story of your sex life to anybody*. Now that everybody's lurid sexual exploits are in the public domain, you can't impress your associates with yours anyway, and Mr. Omnipotence and his wife may be a pair of gold-seal prudes.

14

Going Up the Ladder on Your Back

Who's she *sleeping* with? Who's she *been* sleeping with? Has she been everybody's darling along the way? Or is she the personal property of you-know-who?

Point out almost any woman as a smashing success, and these are the questions that instantly start popping up. Even if she's older than fungus, even though she may look like a near relative of King Kong, men and women who are less successful than she is will console themselves and each other with vocal conjectures about her sex habits, on and off the job.

The only speculation likely to take precedence over this one has to do with money. How much is she getting? Has she always made a pile of dough, or is this the first time she ever saw a decent paycheck? Is she stashing the stuff away? Or is she blowing it, surreptitiously but steadily, on some happy fellow who hates working?

The ties between sex and money have always been stronger than most people are willing to admit, but evidence abounds that money is the long-sought aphrodisiac —the only one that really works. These sex-money ties may be the secret conduits of the deathless notion that any woman who has made it big has made it first with a very big man. The idea that she might possibly achieve something on her own goes against the code of the hills. All this may be one reason why wives don't believe their husbands when they swear they were working late. And why husbands don't actually expect them to believe it either.

It is, of course, entirely possible for a skillful girl to go up the ladder on her back. I know a few very successful career women who have pulled off this acrobatic feat with the ease of a circus superstar. But these are the ones who also knew how to handle themselves on every rung of that ladder. Exquisitely. Maybe they did get their first breaks in bed, but they were smart enough to make all the right moves when they got up. In all probability these women would have been tremendously successful anyway. Maybe not as soon. Maybe sooner. Who knows?

The ones to be "more pitited than censured" are the bubbleheads who have believed what they read in the hard-breathing novels and magazines and decided that the sure way to the boardroom was through the bedroom. Our overheated sexual climate has convinced them that a few spirited romps in the right bedrooms will guarantee them vice-presidencies with plenty of luscious perks by the first of the year at the latest. There are always a few male sex hounds around the office to fan the fiction. To promise them anything—and give them the proverbial Arpège.

A woman I know who has plenty of little Arpège-like goodies and is still earning coolie wages sums it up very simply. She parrots a philosophy long expressed by men: "I enjoy sex. But the screwing I got wasn't worth the screwing I got."

The idea that a woman around the office is there to double in dalliance is as old-fashioned as it is old. My Aunt Freda says that in 1916 she made a thirty-six-hour trip to St. Louis to take a job "trimming hats" for a man she had never met. They had made a deal through the mail, and she says she stepped over the maimed-though-not-quite-dead bodies of her father and brother to get on the train. Her mother and sister were cheering her on. She arrived in St. Louis with cinders in her hair, stars in her eyes and a crushing disappointment ahead. It was made immediately clear to her that hat trimming was only an incidental part of the job—the part intended to hide the real purpose of her employment from the hat man's wife. My aunt, who has always had an abundance of moxie, informed her employer that if she had to make a living "doing *that,*" she could get more money for it in Mississippi—and wouldn't have to sew tacky flowers on cheap hats either! She caught the next train back home, sans stars and with the first trip's cinders still under her own flowered hat.

Blocking That Pass

Today it is mainly the men at the lower levels of management who pursue female associates. Most of the upper echelon are so plagued with problems that they don't have much energy or inclination left for sideline romancing. When I told a client of mine that I was writing a chapter about sex in business, he looked bewildered. *"Sex?"* he said, in a small, hollow voice. "Could you spell that please? Oh! I remember now. All I can tell you is I hope the heaviest sexual demand made on me this whole week will be an invitation to a porno movie. That will be easy to turn down!"

Apparently, however, there are still some old-timers around who feel that women in their employ should be available to them for exhilarating entertainment after hours. They may even look upon this as an extra-special treat for the girls, especially when drinks and dinner are thrown in. I recently heard a young woman at a career counseling session complain that she had been fired because she had not gone along with the game plan her boss had devised for an out-of-town business meeting they attended together. "The old fool took it for granted that I was going to bed with him," she said. "He just came to my room at midnight with his travel kit that had God knows what in it—like it was all settled. I told him I wouldn't dream of letting him touch me, and—can you believe it?—he fired me! Right there. Even though I explained to him that he was old enough to be my father."

Old enough to be her father! Of course, the man fired her. She had destroyed his male ego by handing him an image of himself he couldn't bear to look at. Neither could he bear to look at *her* ever again. So she lost a job she really wanted to keep and had a tough time getting another. The reference her former boss gave her suggested that she was uncooperative and "difficult." It is illegal, of course, to fire a woman on grounds of sexual denial, but there are plenty of grounds that *are* legal, and a legitimate one can always be found.

The woman I know who used the horizontal approach to business most successfully was known around the office as Passionata Springs. Passionata had a strong libido which she indulged at first with four young men (yes, *four!*) at her own job level, in addition to her first husband. After a year of this she moved along to a triumvirate in middle management, then divorced her husband and went to another company, where she practiced her sorcery only on the vigorous and youthful boss. Then she really got smart and graduated to *his* boss, a client of his who was another dynamic type with a sound heart and iron constitution. Today, she heads a multimillion-dollar empire and does not speak to any of the four men who, in their youth, helped her make it through the night, the afternoon, the morning, Shrove Tuesday, whatever! One of them works for her now, but when she meets him in the elevator or lobby of their building, there is no flicker of recognition. From him either. He says he remembers what not to remember and pretends they're both somebody else.

Passionata's horizontal climb to glory could not easily be duplicated today. Most of it took place in the 1960s, just before the dawn of the new sexual freedom, women's liberation and the tough new competitiveness in business. Back then it was still possible for Helen Gurley Brown to shock people with books called *Sex and the Single Girl* and *Sex and the Office,* the latter distinguished only by detailed instructions on how to conduct a "matinee."

"Matinee" is a word still used by some New Yorkers to indicate love on one's lunch hour. In Los Angeles it's called a nooner, and in Mississippi a mistake. My compatriots don't believe in rushing things.

As I recall it, Mrs. Brown's matinee guide was enough to kill any romance. For one thing, it imposed burdens on the woman that could get Mrs. Brown murdered at the next liberation rally. The female matinee star was supposed to do the shopping the day before, cook the lunch the night before, lay in the booze and vino the week before and rush out of the office in time to arrive at the apartment twenty minutes ahead of her costar. Then all she had to do was change into something sexy, mix the drinks, meet him at the door with a warm heart and a chilly martini, serve the lunch—and, if she hadn't dropped dead of exhaustion by then, go into her Du Barry Number.

She also had to remember to wear no perfume (it might still cling to her partner when he went home to his wife), examine him and his clothes for telltale signs like lipstick, check him and herself out for wet locks after showering and be sure to wear the same clothes back to the office that she had on that morning. According to Mrs. Brown, a noontime wardrobe switch is a dead giveaway that you've just struggled in from a big matinee—

even if you really had to go home and change because you stepped in a manhole or got run down by a taxi.

So Let Them Talk—They Will Anyway

The Boss Lady isn't likely to do anything at lunchtime that will get her back to the office late, exhausted and incapable of coping with the afternoon's problems. If she has changed clothes, it is probably because of some new or forgotten plans after work. At any rate, her sex life is usually a lively topic of discussion, regardless of age or general appearance. The guessing game about the unmarried Boss Lady goes from lesbianism to frigidity to bitterness over a lost lover to assumption that she's involved with a man who is a no-no because he's either too big or too insignificant to talk about. The married Boss Lady, in turn, is subject to surmise that her husband is an underachieving earner, an overachieving lover (embarrassing her with the pursuit of all her best friends and worst enemies) or a convenient cover-up for her own lurid amours. The divorcée gets the worst of both worlds in the yakking about what caused the breakup. No Boss Lady should let any of this disturb her. The talk comes with the territory and means nothing at all, except that she's the focus of interest.

One of the most popular stories about successful businesswomen is told so often by young men in their employ that I wonder how the young fellows have the cheek to repeat it. There are two standard versions. One: "When she hired me, she said, 'By the way, how are you in bed? I'll expect to see you after hours a couple of times a week.' I needed the job, so I took it. But how does a guy handle *that?*" Two: "She asked me to come to her apartment for dinner so we could talk about the project quietly, and after a few drinks she said, 'Have you ever had a *real* woman? I mean a *real* one! I could teach you things, baby, about this company and a lot more. . . .' It frightened me so badly that I ran out of there without dinner, and the next day she acted as if nothing had happened!"

Something like that could have happened to a young man here and there—and possibly did—but there is no denying that the story, in all its rich variations, has become popular legend. The young men who parrot it probably don't even realize that they are compensating for the conflicts they feel about working for a woman. The ones who actually do stumble into such an experience should know that the fictional stories on the subject are so familiar that nobody's going to believe their true report. Boasting about it to anybody except the most naive and inexperienced employees on the premises will open up a gap in their credibility the width of Grand Canyon.

When a Boss Lady gets romantically involved with the Boss Man, there can be hell to pay all around, and it's a safe bet that she's the one who'll do the paying. I know an exceptionally capable woman who was already a top executive when the company that employed her was bought by a conglomerate. She and the conglomerate head immediately responded to each other on a deeper level than those touched by their respective jobs. He lived in California with his wife, she lived in New York with her cat and they were soon living with each other all over the country every chance they got. After two years of this she insisted that he get a divorce and marry her. He got the divorce, all right, but decided not to get married again. Instead, he quit his job as head of the conglomerate and went to live in the Orient, to paint and meditate, assuring her that she'd "be okay at the company." She was left to the tender mercies of the male executives who had been scared witless of her while she was the acknowledged darling of Mr. Omnipotence. Needless to say, she was fired before he was even on the plane to Hong Kong—and guess what the references written for her by Mr. O's successor say? The last time I heard of her, she had so much time on her hands that she was thinking of getting a second cat.

It was a little different for a younger woman I know whom I'll call Maggie Greenspan. Maggie was in minor management when she caught the eye (the roving one), of her company's president. At first it was great for her career. He made her the director of a division, a job that she was eminently capable of handling and might have been promoted to anyway. She was so overcome with gratitude, to say nothing of the unexpected glory, that she divorced her husband, throwing herself wholeheartedly into both halves of the situation. But the romantic half soon took over, and she and the president took longer and longer lunch hours until the board chairman decided that Maggie was interfering with *el presidente*'s work and insisted that she be fired. Her paramour wished her luck but was so alarmed by the lecture he got from the chairman that he didn't even answer requests he got for a reference from companies where Maggie was being considered. The last time I heard of him, the alarm had passed, and he was repeating the whole process with another young woman at his company. Maggie is back at the typewriter, pounding out statistical reports and hating it. She called up her ex-husband once but, when a woman answered, hung up.

The distinguished anthropologist Margaret Mead sees sex at the office as a sort of corporate incest. Speaking in September 1977 at a meeting of businesswomen held at the UN, Dr. Mead declared that "we've got to do something about sex if we're going to have women in business." She said that like the family, the modern corporation must develop incest taboos. "If we're going to have men and women in business on an equal basis," she continued, "with men over women and women over men, we have to develop decent sex mores. We've got to stop the kind of exploitation that is usual, the young men who prey on older women, the middle-aged men (preying on) younger women, the office wife, the Christmas parties— we're going to have to get rid of this." Dr. Mead explained that mixing sex into the corporate hierarchy breeds trouble: "It's very difficult to run an army if the general is in love with the sergeant." Or if the corporal is having fun in bed with the captain!

Now that blabbing about one's torrid affairs with the famous has become an industry, women who have ascended to high office can expect to become juicy subject matter for the trash writers who are scraping the gutters for new material. We loudly proclaim a new sexual freedom throughout the land. Yet we remain a nation of eager voyeurs, pouring billions each year into the porno press—innocently underwriting all the news that's unfit to print about our heroes and heroines. The show biz superstars flourish on this kind of publicity, but sexual indiscretions among the titans of government, education and commerce have proved disastrous, even for men. Our double standard being what it is, female governors, congresswomen, senators, Cabinet members and corporate presidents cannot hope to get away with erotic high jinks.

So if it appears that you're going to be a Very Big Boss Lady, you'd better be extra-careful where you do your sleeping. It could become a nightmare. You'll hate yourself in the morning, for sure, if you pick up a newspaper or magazine, switch on the radio or telly and find that your little fling (discreet though it might have been) is a delicious topic for public dissection and discussion. The investigative reporters are already mind-blastingly skillful at digging up ancient bones, as well as sweeping fresh dirt out from under the bed. Think how clever they'll be twenty years from now. And watch it!

Of course, sex is always with us, in and out of the office, but it may be helpful to remember these four things:

1. *Going up the ladder on your head may seem more difficult than making the trip on your back, but in the long run it's more emotionally rewarding.* Safer, too, because this year's romance can be next year's disaster. Also, a quarrel on a date only spoils the evening, but when it's carried over into the office, it can spoil a whole program or project.

2. *If you do get involved in an office affair, keep it as inconspicuous as possible.* It does not pay to advertise, especially when the other half is the Boss Man himself. Scaring the daylights out of associates with your paramour power may seem like good, clean fun at the time, but those terrified people have some cruel ways of getting even when the time runs out.

3. *Do not be upset with rumors that you romanced your way to the executive suite, but try not to fuel them either.* An effective female executive almost always goes farther faster than the girl who acts like a card-carrying nymphomaniac.

4. *Learn to turn away unwelcome advances without turning off an important client or associate.* Above all, don't cite his age as an excuse. The only answer that a man can accept without embarrassment is "There's somebody else!" The pressure usually stops cold when you explain that your husband or lover is wildly jealous and would murder any man who so much as looked at you.

15

Join the Club

Okay, you're not a joiner. By nature, neither am I. Until I joined Advertising Women of New York I had never been a member of anything except American Express and the Baptist Church. This was not as smart as I had led myself to believe.

Every industry has its trade organizations. The clubs and associations exist to promote the interests of the industry at large and those of the membership in specific ways. They collect and store information. They conduct studies, prepare reports and make presentations. They conduct programs geared to the problems and opportunities of the field. They "lobby" for the industry in Washington and state capitals. And they can help you in dozens of ways, big and little, to advance your career.

Most people don't know how to use these organizations and shy away from them—fearful that they'll be coerced into doing time-consuming, gratuitous "industry work" and attending another round of those calcifying luncheons, dinners and conventions. Their fears are well founded. The clubs and associations can drive you straight out of your mind with picayune chores and with business-social occasions dull enough to turn the best-padded bottoms and psyches to stone. But they can also save your sanity or even your job by giving you immediate information—important facts and figures from the studies and reports mentioned above. They provide you with opportunities to make valuable contacts, to meet the big guns in your field in person or at least to speak with them on the telephone. And in the process you can become known to people who might otherwise never hear your name. What is perhaps most important of all, they can give you a showcase for your particular talents, a platform for your ideas and opinions, a chance to grow in new directions that will be meaningful to your career.

I didn't know any of this and would not have believed it if anybody had bothered to tell me. I was virtually ordered to join Advertising Women of New York by one of my female bosses who was on the AWNY membership committee and made it abundantly clear that she would be a happier woman if the faithful in her department joined the club. I did, but at first I could only hope that *she* was happier because *I* was miserable about the whole thing. I have a photograph shot at the reception for new members which welcomed me and seven other new recruits. I appear to have been smiling, but I was really gritting my teeth. To make the time spent with the club go faster, I began doing some work for the organization, became interested in its programs, became more and more active in all of them and within a few years became president. It was one of the key developments in my career.

The Army Says, "Never Volunteer"—but You're Not in the Army

Clubs and associations are microcosms of business. Although their purposes do not concern profits, their functions do concern the raising and disbursement of funds. The fund raising is always a problem; disbursement comes naturally to everybody. As in a business, there is always work to be done, but the big difference is that much, most or maybe all of it must be done by volunteers. Volunteers can be wonderful, often acting beyond the call of duty, but the majority of them are not as reliable as paid employees who may suddenly suffer loss of income if they fail to do what is expected of them. Since volunteers are not rewarded with money, any rewards that come to them for effort in their industry come in the form of love, honor and glory. And power!

You acquire power in one of these organizations by contributing time, talent and a lot of hard work. The people who are running them desperately need help they can count on, and if you demonstrate reliable and effective performance, the president and the other officers will welcome you to the fold with joy and thanksgiving, advancing you rapidly through the ranks. Once you become a committee chairman, you must motivate other members to join you in accomplishing whatever it is you hope to do. As you advance in the organization, it's necessary to motivate more and more people at higher levels. And I can tell you from experience that it's easier to write about this than to do it.

Volunteers have a disconcerting way of quitting a job they've taken on without telling you or anybody else they've quit. You get the bad news only at the moment of reckoning when everything is supposed to be ready and in place. The Boss Lady of the project or the whole organization must then (a) do it herself or (b) get somebody else to do it—fast! The smarter she is, the more likely are the chances that she has a close coterie of "faithfuls" around her who are willing to leap into the breach. It is also essential that she have the full support of her company and at least some use of office facilities for the club work she's engaged in. Lacking that, she may be hard pressed to get the job done—particularly when a volunteer has chickened out or become ill at the last minute. The enlightened companies are almost always glad to support the industry activities of a woman in their employ and are grateful that she's willing to make a contribution of time and effort for the benefit of the field.

Women who are active in their industry's coed organizations often complain that the men grab off all the honors and leave them to do the "dirty work," all the piddling little tasks that are the equivalent of dishwashing and vacuuming—if not actually that. "The men take all the interesting jobs and do the things that get their names and pictures in the newspapers," says a young woman in one of the coed clubs. "And we're stuck with the stamp licking, envelope stuffing and all the other little bore chores."

In sexually integrated clubs the old familiar double standard remains in force, and a woman advances in the hierarchy of a coed organization mainly through extra-hard work—and constant vigilance. She goes up only by observing the rules of the game, which continue to be dictated largely by the men. The trick is to learn what the rules are, and that's where the vigilance comes in.

Advertising Women of New York does not have this male supremacy problem. One of the first business organizations for women in the United States, it was founded in 1913 by Christine Fredericks, whose other achievements included authorship of the first singing commercial and raising the kitchen sink eighteen inches higher. She got $5 for the singing commercial and deserves sainthood for the sink raising. Until Christine came along, the kitchen sink was way down there on the floor, where the European men who had designed the thing had put it. Since the men didn't wash the dishes, they weren't getting the backaches bending way down there. Any groans of "Oh, my aching back!" emanating from the kitchen were dismissed with an understanding shrug as "female trouble." Now that men in many households share the dishwashing, they too should murmur a few sudsy words of thanks to Christine.

This feisty woman not only raised the kitchen sink but also raised unholy hell with her husband because she and her women friends were barred from a lecture they wanted to hear at an all-male advertising organization which he served as president. He finally relented and agreed to let Christine and her friends come to the lecture but said they'd have to sit behind a curtain where the men could not see them. That did it! Christine told her husband what he could do with his curtain, and while the marriage survived, his plans for women's attendance at his meetings did not. She got her friends together and assumed leadership in forming Advertising Women of New York. Thereafter they booked speakers for their own meetings, magnanimously letting men attend in full view of the membership. It should be said to the credit of husband Fredericks, who was an important magazine editor of the day, that he helped AWNY book the speakers they wanted to hear. Christine (who died only a few years ago in California) always said that the dear man really wanted to be helpful to women but felt constrained to observe the traditions of his own sex.

It May Be a Bore, but It Can Also Cure Headaches

Your industry's trade organizations may bore you from time to time with speakers who are less than inspirational, but at other times they may hand you an unexpected nugget that can help you solve a hairy problem or perform a visible and/or laudable feat for yourself and/or your company.

One of the first jobs I took on at AWNY was on the program committee—a fortunate choice dictated more by boredom than wisdom. Since I was expected to attend programs, I felt motivated to try to make them interesting, and I decided that the career subjects which appealed to me would spark interest in other members, too. We set about creating a slate of activities highlighting areas of the advertising business that were of special concern at the moment, putting emphasis on new techniques, ideas and theories in art, copy and graphics, and some very exciting programs resulted. Not so exciting, but extremely meaningful, were the legislative programs which acquired luster when we took them to Washington, met the President and assorted dignitaries in the Senate, Congress and Cabinet and observed the workings of government on the inside, which is the side that seems to count most.

One of the most effective club presidents I ever knew was Jean Middlebrook of the Women's Advertising Club of Chicago, who now heads Middlebrook Enterprises, a flourishing travel agency on Chicago's Rush Street. Jean could get the club membership to work like galley slaves. Of the 260 dues-paying members in the organization, 243 were actively engaged in committee work—and I do mean *actively!* I once phoned Jean at her office and, learning that she was sick in bed with a cold, called her at home. Six members were holding a committee meeting in her living room during their lunch hour!

I asked Jean how she kept up such a high degree of enthusiasm, and she said it was simple. "Most of those women are frustrated at the office," she explained, "because they're stuck in routine jobs that don't really utilize their capabilities. The club projects let them function at full capacity, and they're delighted. They are deeply involved because they feel a proprietary interest that's lacking at the office. These industry projects are *theirs,* so they're willing to work on them nights, weekends and holidays." Jean joined the Women's Advertising Club of Chicago as an outlet for her own supercharged energies, and she says that the contacts she made there have been of inestimable value in her own firm.

Young businesswomen who become active in clubs and associations can learn some things that will speed them along to the executive suite. They can not only plug into valuable inside information about their industry but also learn how to speak up in public and how to express their ideas clearly and in a manner that will gain acceptance.

Patricia Martin, a district chairman of the American Advertising Federation, says that there is a tremendous surge of interest in club work among younger women today. "When I first got involved in industry organizations, most of the women who belonged to them were approaching middle age or already there," says Pat. "Now there are young people all over the place—women in their twenties and thirties who are eager to learn all they can and share their own talents with the industry where they hope to achieve success."

Pat is director of creative services for a division of a large pharmaceutical house (Warner-Lambert) and is impressed with the enthusiasm of young women who are being employed by her own company and others in the field. "These girls have an entirely different outlook," she observes. "They expect to move along in their jobs and are willing to put out extra effort to do it. They show up at the big conventions, and when they get there, they spend their time at meetings and information-exchange sessions instead of sitting around the hospitality suites drinking Bloody Marys."

While young women today are inclined to be more forthright and confident than their predecessors, they are still at a disadvantage in being heard, because men remain more attentive to other men in business situations than to women. So the experience you get in expressing yourself at a club meeting can be beneficial to you at the office when you need to get and hold the attention of a group that isn't particularly interested in listening to anybody, especially women. Moreover, the executive woman can create valuable publicity for herself and her company by speaking at luncheons, dinners, conventions, business forums and educational institutions. All these groups are constantly beating the bushes for good speakers, and now a woman speaker is practically mandatory for every program committee, along with the requisite black.

I have always had an unnaturally keen interest in speeches and speech makers and as a child was enchanted by the fulsome rhetoric of the Mississippi politicians and the Baptist preachers who threatened us with hellfire and damnation at the annual revival meetings that were always held in August, when the Deep South heat made hellfire seem more like a promise than a threat. I myself began making speeches in college but gave it up when my undergraduate rhetoric proved offensive to the administration it attacked. I was given the message that I might be happier elsewhere. I left quietly and thereafter, with superhuman effort, kept my mouth shut.

In Advertising Women of New York I learned to speak up again. I had been intimidated for a long time by New York and my overconfident Madison Avenue associates and had experienced some painful difficulties in getting my bearings. At AWNY I had to learn how to get my ideas across, how to conduct a meeting and eventually how to hold the attention of a huge audience. I made my first professional speech at a convention of the American Advertising Federation in Boston, which I attended as an officer of AWNY. I beat my typewriter to bits on the text, which presented my "Nine Commandments for Women in Business," and was rewarded with a standing ovation plus a "pickup" on the Associated Press wire. The AP quotes were printed in more than six hundred newspapers in the United States and translated for newspapers in Germany, Italy and France. The quotes were the Nine Commandments, and I believe that they still apply today.

1. Thou shalt try harder; thou need not be only number two.

2. Thou shalt know when to zip thy lip and listen quietly.

3. Thou shall not attempt to hide behind thine own petticoat.

4. Thou shalt speak softly and carry no stick, except lipstick.

5. Thou shalt serve thy lady boss as graciously as thou servest any man.

6. When success cometh, thou shall not get too big for thy bustle.

7. Thou shalt watch thy language; there may be gentlemen present.

8. Thou shall not match martinis with the men.

9. Thou shalt save thy sex appeal for after five, even though thy C cup runneth over.

The effect of the response was intoxicating, and since then I have spoken in every major city in the United States and some of the smaller communities. The two most difficult audiences I ever faced were made up of those who knew me best. One was in my hometown, and the other was at a luncheon of the Greenwich Village Chamber of Commerce in Manhattan, where I found myself pontificating to neighbors—the druggist around the corner from where I live, the dentist in the building next door, the captain of our police precinct and assorted others who know me as a customer, a patient or complainer. When I was finished, the druggist came over and said, "I just want you to know the Eighth Street Pharmacy is proud of you!" It was a fine moment.

Nobody Wants to Listen—You Have to Make Them Hear You

If you are the woman speaker chosen for an industry occasion, look on it as an opportunity rather than a chore.

Don't underestimate it, even though you may decide that it's a "nothing" event that you were a fool to associate yourself with. Once you've agreed to do it, live up to your commitment and give it your best shot. There are people counting on you, and besides, you never know who may be listening who'll be important to you someday, somewhere. Because you *are* a woman, your audience is apt to be more attentive—at the start anyway—and more critical as well. Holding their attention is the whole ball game. Be prepared. Find out first of all whom you'll be talking to—age, sex, special interests, particular sensitivities—and what they expect to get out of a message from you.

Unless you're the kind of speaker who enjoys "stirring up the animals," who goes on deliberately to pick a fight, try to get the audience on your side in the first two minutes. Don't tell them how hard you've worked on this presentation or what a tough time you've had getting here or how much you gave up to do this arduous deed because nobody gives a damn. Most of them don't want to hear a speech anyway, a lot of them are tired, restless, bored or a little of each, and a few will be half-smashed. You may safely assume that they aren't dying to listen to another speaker and that because you're a woman, they'll probably think you can't tell them much anyway. Maybe you're in no mood to assume any of those things, but no matter how confident you feel, don't wing it. Have a written text or a full outline before you, even if you don't intend to use it. You may think you come off okay ad-libbing it, but you'll never get a reputation as a red-hot speaker just getting up and saying whatever pops into your head. Try to look and sound as if that's what you're doing, but think your speech through thoroughly—even your wickedly clever ad libs!—before you march bravely up to the lectern. Men can sometimes get away with a slapdash performance on grounds of being too busy, but a woman can never get away with it on any grounds. It's that old double standard again.

From Mike Fright to Mike Fever

Almost everybody is subject to mike fright in one form or another, but try not to let it dismay you. It can actually be good for your performance because it gets the adrenaline going, revs you up. Just don't let your jitters become so violently apparent that your audience gets involved in them and starts shaking along with you. Do not make the mistake of trying to steady your nerves by overfortifying yourself with uppers, downers or the thoughtfully provided beverages of your zealous hosts. Don't rely on any fortification except a carefully researched and skillfully put-together text. If you're not a writer, get one, but be sure to familiarize yourself with the pearly words and convert them to your own style. Rehearse, too. Remember that you don't have a right to bore your audience, however gifted and famous you may be or however insignificant they may be.

Using slides at the beginning can help you get over your speaker's nerves until you get used to being "on." With the houselights down, you can feel blissfully hidden, and by the time they go back up you may even be enjoying yourself. Your mike fright may even turn into a roaring case of mike fever once you get the audience listening and responding in all the right places. Just be sure that any slides you use are meaningful, that they actually underline the points you're making and that they can be seen by everybody in the house.

The last point means getting to the room where you're going to speak in time to check out the positioning of the screen and the functioning of the audiovisual equipment. All audiovisual machines have a soul of their own. That soul, unfortunately for you, is demonic and, given the slightest chance, will throw you. Test every piece of equipment involved. Don't rely on the engineers, and try to say something cheerful that will get them on your side when they start muttering about "jittery dames." When you go on, you're in their power, and if things get fouled up, you're the one who'll be on the spot. If, in spite of all your checking, the microphone starts to squeal, or the slides go on upside down and backward, or the film projector starts blurring or groaning, don't panic. Stop and wait patiently while the equipment is being fixed. Have a few friendly little jokes ready that do not berate or ridicule the men who are doing the fixing. Make them mad at this point, and they'll see to it that nothing gets fixed except your wagon. When the meeting is over, be sure to thank them, no matter how badly they screwed things up. You may be back someday.

Speaking of gratitude, when you become a boss or *the* boss in your organization, be sure to thank anybody who does anything for the cause—promptly and warmly. Write a note and send it to the office of the person you're thanking. Take time to make it the kind of message that can be duplicated and relayed to Mr. Omnipotence there. He may be glad to know that the person you're thanking is importantly involved in the business community, and she may be more inclined to take on additional activities in the club. See to it, too, that your guest speakers get the red-carpet treatment. Give them a memento of the occasion—something impressive that can become part of their offices. If they're from out of town, have someone meet them at the airport and escort them to their hotel. Making a speech is hard work and deserves a show of appreciation.

I will always have a soft spot in my heart and head for Mansfield, Ohio, because the ad club there emblazoned six giant billboards with WELCOME, JO FOX-

WORTH! in letters a foot and a half high. The same thing happened in Buffalo, New York, and in Wilmington, Delaware, and the experience was so exhilarating each time that I'll speak my brains out in those cities any time those head-turning people ask me. On the other hand, I will never go back to another Ohio city, which shall be as nameless as it deserves, and I go out of my way to advise all my speaking friends to avoid it, too. The people there were so thoroughly matter-of-fact about my visit that they forgot to tell me the meeting place had been changed, and I had to track down the new luncheon site, unassisted.

Joining the club may not sound like fun, especially if it's sexually segregated, but if you put real effort into the work, the rewards can be lovely. Advertising Women of New York honored me twice with their presidency and twice with their Advertising Woman of the Year award. They also made me their candidate for the same award on a national basis, and the American Advertising Federation presented me that one in Miami, where I was the happiest woman on or off the beach. I even forgot all the committee heads who had quit without letting me know.

If you do decide to become active in one or more of your industry's organizations, and I hope you will, keep the following points in mind:

1. *Get your company's full blessing at the start.* If Mr. Omnipotence doesn't know what the organization does, fill him in—with emphasis on the professional activities. Underscore the fact that the social events are fund raisers to support the programs that are beneficial to his business. This will help you get the endorsement and backing you need from your company.

2. *Volunteer your services on some highly visible projects that will "showcase" your talents to the club and the business community.* Don't hesitate to pitch in

on the drudgery stuff, too—the things that nobody wants to do. This will endear you to the people who are running the show and make them so tearfully grateful that they'll be overjoyed to give you the jobs in the club you really want.

3. *Get involved in some kinds of work that you haven't been doing.* This will permit you to grow in new directions and develop other talents that you've set aside or maybe didn't even know you had. In AWNY I did writing that had nothing to do with the ad copy I wrote for a living and, in the course of turning out texts for industry articles and speeches, became a columnist for the trade bible of my industry, *Advertising Age.* I also dusted off a long-neglected penchant for speech making and embarked on an avocation as public speaker which has permitted me to see every major city in the United States, including Honolulu, at no expense to myself.

4. *Surround yourself with enthusiastic, conscientious workers who can be relied on to do not only their own jobs in the club but those of the sudden flameouts.*

5. *Make all the friends you can in your own city and others throughout the industry.* These contacts can be enormously valuable to you in getting needed information in a hurry—or in getting another job.

16

You and Me and the ERA

Any Boss Lady who values her status concerns herself with the political and social issues that affect the quality of life beyond her own office and household. Few such issues have been more loudly hymned or roundly damned than the Equal Rights Amendment, which, I suffer to say, I had been pleased to ignore until I got a call from Advertising Women of New York asking me to serve on that organization's ERA committee. I didn't want to do it. The committee was supposed to produce advertising and promotion materials directed toward the amendment's ratification, and I wasn't a bit sure that ERA was a good idea. But it is very difficult for me to say no to anything AWNY asks me to do, so after voicing strong misgivings, I reluctantly agreed to carry a spear as a professional.

The most active members of the committee, those who really cracked into the project and worked at it, all were high-voltage women who have plenty to do besides sit in committee meetings pondering the wondrous ways of the American electorate. They were: Rena Bartos, vice-president of the J. Walter Thompson Company, the lofty advertising agency which (after Japan's Dentsu) is the world's largest; Joan Hogan, director of research for Condé Nast publications (*Vogue, Glamour,* etc.); Marcia Allen, at the time editor and co-publisher of *Where* magazine, which is distributed in major hotels throughout the country; Jane Creel, director of consumer affairs for Lever Brothers; Jean Rindlaub, now a busy advertising consultant and a retired vice-president of the giant ad agency whose name is said to sound like a trunk falling downstairs, Batten, Barton, Durstine & Osborn; and Barbara Hunter, executive vice-president of Dudley-Anderson-Yutzy, the huge public relations firm that (among other things) calls the tune for Chiquita Banana and the rest of "The Banana Bunch."

It was a lively committee. Needless to say, all these women achieved their prominent positions under the existing laws of the day and will continue to flourish whether ERA is ratified or relegated to the congressional trash heap. How much faster they'd have got there or how much farther they could have gone given equal opportunities is useless conjecture. The point is that beyond the mid-stripe in their own careers, they were willing to spend weary hours in an effort that stood to benefit other people more than themselves. It is the Boss Ladies and Boss Men of tomorrow who will be helped most by their work. And that impressed me.

In my own defense, I must say that the main reason I was reluctant to become a member of the committee was that like hundreds of thousands of other people, I didn't know much about it. Few pieces of legislation have been as poorly presented to the public. Its champions have been depressingly ineffective in communicating ERA's far-reaching benefits, making it easy for the opposition to becloud it with trivia.

The Carry Nation of the anti-ERA forces is a female politician named Phyllis Schlafly who, apparently, hopes to ride the women's liberation backlash into the United States Congress. Mrs. Schlafly has twice lost her bid for a congressional seat, first in 1952 and again in 1970. Two years after her second defeat at the polls, she discovered in the Equal Rights Amendment an issue that she obviously looks upon as a vote-getting gold mine. In 1972 she devoted the text of her extreme right-wing newsletter to a blast against the proposed legislation, and the response to her garbled report on ERA seems to have convinced her that here was an issue that could generate a publicity windfall for her continuing political campaign.

Like the redoubtable Mrs. Nation, Schlafly swings a mean hatchet, flailing away against ERA with emotional rhetoric that (thanks, largely, to the ineffectiveness of ERA's organized proponents) reduces the issue largely to a potty and foxhole argument—sounding dire warnings about what will happen to women in foxholes with men in wartime and in public toilets with them any time. This, of course, ignores these facts:

1. *His and Her Foxholes.* ERA will not draft women into the armed forces. But under the laws that already exist Congress may, in the event of military necessity, draft women as well as men. It should be noted that there are hundreds of noncombat jobs in every branch of the armed forces, and ERA will permit women to get a fair share of these, along with the considerable benefits that accrue from military service.

2. *His and Her Public Potties.* Men and women have been using the same toilet facilities on planes, trains and other public carriers as long as these conveyances have been in existence. Surely the public plumbing in other places can be arranged so that it may be used without loss of privacy and without any of the other dark consequences that have been suggested.

ERA will not be a deciding factor in the battle of the sexes in or out of foxholes, in or out of the john, but it will make discrimination on grounds of gender more difficult and may even make some of the people who practice discrimination as uncomfortable as discrimination makes those, who, unavoidably, are its victims. Moreover, it can help make it as gauche to engage in casual or merry put-downs of women as it now is to say "kike," "wop" or "nigger."

Oddly, a great many men and women who profess

total endorsement of the female quest for a better break either actively oppose ERA or express vague doubts about its efficacy. Like me before I got the call from AWNY, they don't know much about it and are, therefore, jittery about what its effects may be. The lesbian and pro-abortion groups have obscured the amendment still further and give new ammunition to the alarmists, who declare that ERA in particular and the women's movement in general can only be destructive to American family life —which, according to them, is in tatters already.

Any cry of alarm about the degeneration of the family hits the Boss Lady where she lives because it preys on the guilt feelings that so many working women have. Writing in the December 1977 issue of *Family Circle* Earl C. Gottschalk Jr. said that "the anxious hand-wringing over the decline of the American family is absolute baloney!" Gottschalk cited new research by Dr. Mary Jo Bane of Wellesley College which revealed that "mothers who stayed home to tend their children 100 years ago frequently ignored them during a long day's work, probably giving them less attention than working mothers do today." My own acquaintance with career women who have children certainly bears this out, in sharp contradiction to the current cataract of magazine and newspaper articles mourning the death of family life.

One Boss Lady I know told me that her teenage son and daughter, after reading a succession of these pieces, confronted her with the news that they would like her to quit her job and "be in the kitchen baking cookies" when they came home from school—the way mothers were in the "good-old-days," the 1890s. She listened carefully, then offered to make a deal with them. She would quit her job and pursue the household duties of a nineteenth-century mother if they would adopt the habits and manners of nineteenth-century children. They immediately understood the changes this would cause in their own pursuit of happiness and sheepishly withdrew the request. They acknowledged that the time their mother spends with them is prime time, and the cookie baking could well be left to Pepperidge Farms.

Nineteenth-century customs and attitudes were great —for the nineteenth century—but we have entered the last quarter of the twentieth century with entirely different needs and desires. Only the dreaming remains the same—to be all that we can be, a dream that is as meaningful to women as it is to any man. The law ought to allow at least that. If necessary, even command it!

The Boss Lady has a special obligation to the human community. It has been said so often that women have to work twice as hard to get half as much as the men do that both sexes have come to expect it. While I hope this is among today's vanishing attitudes, I know for sure that another adage still applies: "If you want to get something done, give the job to somebody who's too busy to do it."

That's what happened with the ERA committee of AWNY. We prepared brochures, newspaper ads, magazine ads, radio scripts and television boards to help spread the word that ERA means only what it says: "Equality of rights under the law shall not be denied or abridged by the United States or by any State on account of sex."

By the time this book is published ERA may be history, but it will still be enormously important for any Boss Lady to remember the following points:

1. *Don't let the Phyllis Schlaflys of the world trick you into thinking with your gonads.* If you've been blessed with a mind good enough for you to become a Boss Lady, accept the pleasure of making it up right there in your head.

2. *Don't duck political issues because you don't*

like politics. Political issues affect your own status in the world and everybody else's, so how can you possibly say, as all too many people do, that you're not concerned?

3. *Get the facts—all of them.* Don't rely on the information that has been filtered through the opinions and personal interests of somebody else.

4. *Even if it's raining or snowing, get to the polls and vote.* It took 114 years for women to win the constitutional right to cast a ballot, and it is shocking to realize that only a small percentage of the female electorate bothers to exercise this hard-won franchise. True, not that many men exercise it either, but unfortunate though that is, at least they've had the right long enough to take it for granted. Even so, a great many more men than women vote; this says something we shouldn't have to hear about the willingness of the sexes to accept responsibility.

5. *If you really believe in a cause, support it.* Work for it. And don't hesitate to express your opinion. Notice how many Boss Ladies do. Should your business associates disagree with your point of view, see to it that they get all the facts on your side of the story—tactfully. Don't try to rub their noses in strawberry if what they go for is vanilla. They do have a right to their opinions, and you can find plenty of people to offend without stepping on the blue suede shoes of someone who can raise your pay, promote you—or pass you by.

17

Two Against the World

Until inflation met women's liberation, the working wife and her husband often had to do some fancy explaining to keep the world from thinking what it often thought already: (a) that he was what my grandmother called a poor provider; (b) that she was a spark-shooting neurotic, a malcontent set against man, nature and, possibly, God; (c) that they were both adolescent in their expectations of life in general and marriage in particular.

Some of yesterday's husbands were downright edgy about such situations. Now most of them not only welcome the idea of a second income brought home by the wife but actively expect it. This attitude is especially prevalent among young college men. Surveys conducted on the campuses of universities and colleges in all part of the country show that among a very large percentage of the male students, their planning for the future includes the earnings of a wife. One of my favorite recent cartoons pictured a young man in a singles bar, resisting as his buddies attempted to propel him toward a cluster of girls at the other end of the room. He was saying, "Nuh-uh. You go ahead. I'm waiting for a girl to come in here carrying a briefcase!"

Newsweek magazine reported in 1977 that 57.7 percent of the nation's working women are married, totaling twenty-two million. Obviously, economic necessity is involved in a substantial number of these instances. Incomes of the working wives' husbands break down like this: 14.6 percent earn less than $7,000 a year, 11.4

percent earn $7,000 to $10,000 and the largest segment of all, 31.7 percent—more than $10,000. Among the working wives whose husbands are in the more than $10,000 bracket it is assumed that at least part of the second income goes into discretionary purchases and/or savings earmarked for specific goals: college for the children, a new or expanded home, retirement or maybe a family business.

Naturally the households where both parents bolt out to business every day are apt to be disaster areas unless they are organized differently from those managed by a full-time housewife. With or without children, the job of keeping a home or apartment running with a reasonable degree of comfort, cleanliness and efficiency is too arduous and time-consuming for a working wife without help—and as many a couple has discovered, the cost of housekeeping help in the current market can be prohibitive. The woman who goes to work in the hope of easing the family financial crunch is often shocked to learn how much it costs to support a job. By the time she has plunked down money for clothes, transportation, lunch out and the services of people to do the housework and baby-sitting her salary has often disappeared, and she may even wind up with a deficit!

The cost of "job maintenance" is what some husbands cite as a reason for wanting their wives to stay at home, and the cost of employing outside cleaning, cooking and baby-sitting services is what some wives cite as a reason for demanding pay at the going hourly rate for their own housework!

At any rate, the wife with a career of her own is now an accepted social phenomenon and a continuing source of problems in many marriages. As long as her job exists as an adjunct to his, the problems are minimized. But when it becomes as meaningful to her as his job is to him, there's trouble in paradise. The question is no longer "Who's keeping the store?" It's become "Who's keeping the house?"

Some of the young women on the way up—and their husbands—indicate that it's no bed of roses. Arriving at an equitable distribution of household responsibilities requires patience, understanding, generosity and tact, on both sides.

Take this case: Karen Worden, a young sales executive in New York, married David Anderson, a chemical engineer. "First there was the problem of my name," Karen says. "I wanted to keep it for business reasons because it was known to my clientele, and changing everybody's records was a bit of a nuisance. However, it was important to David for me to be Mrs. Anderson instead of Ms. Worden, and since it didn't matter all that much to me, I made the change, notifying everybody I do business with.

"Then there was the problem of all those day-to-day chores around the apartment. David is a super guy, but he grew up in a home where the men had everything done for them. The clean clothes and delicious meals just materialized, like magic. His mother was a full-time housewife who ran things superbly, and he apparently believed that things like toilet tissue and toothpaste grew in the bathroom. It honestly didn't occur to him that somebody had to go out and get them and put them where they belong.

"When it developed that he thought I could keep my job and do all the cooking, cleaning and shopping, too, I began to complain. Friction over things like this can, of course, spoil the great things about a relationship, and he didn't think we should even have to talk about anything so mundane. After all, a discussion about dishwashing and the laundry is pretty unromantic stuff!"

Unromantic, yes. But so are dirty clothes and dirty

dishes. Karen and David are gradually working things out, but both acknowledge that it has been a struggle. "When I finally got through to him with the message that I could *not* be a full-time housewife and a full-time career woman, too," Karen says, "we went through another stage almost as bad. He said, 'Okay, Karen, I'll help. Just ask me!' Well, that's no good either. That makes me a beggar or at least means that he's doing me a favor when he goes out and gets the toothpaste or goes in and does the dishes—after I've had a rough day at the office and then cooked dinner. We're gradually getting around to a fair division of chores, but it hasn't been easy."

Joann Paulsen, a twenty-four-year-old media planner, reports a different experience with husband, Michael Rooney, who is a young executive with Collins & Aikman, the giant textile company. When she and Michael were married, he had no objection to her keeping her own name in business, and he expected to take over half of the household chores.

"Neither of us likes housework," Joann says, "but there are certain things that each of us loathes especially. Fortunately they're not the same things."

Michael chimes in with: "Yeah, I can't stand to take out the garbage, and she can't stand to clean the bathroom. So *she* takes out the garbage—which she doesn't mind—and I keep the bathroom clean—which I don't mind. It was a bit of a blow to find out about scrubbing the john, though. I sort of thought those things cleaned themselves, like they do in the ads on television. But I found out that somebody has to scrub them down, and at our apartment that's me."

Joann and Michael share the dishwashing detail, and since they both like to cook, they take turns preparing dinner. They pool their earnings and do the bill paying together.

Among the wives who are ten years or so older than

Joann and Karen and are very high-powered executives indeed, the problems are different. A couple I'll call Fran Brewer and Ralph Sims are both editors, he with a major metropolitan newspaper, she with a weekly news-magazine. "We are both in crisis businesses," she says, "and sometimes hardly see each other for a week. During those stretches, we may be so immersed in our business projects that we work in separate rooms and never have discussions with each other about what we're working on because it's confidential. We almost always have dinner out, but we both like to cook and love being in the kitchen together. A cleaning woman comes in twice a week to keep the apartment in order, and we divide the shopping. Usually, when we entertain, it's a small dinner for, maybe, six special friends. For those occasions, he does the shopping, I do the cooking, and we load the dishwasher together."

Tina Santi, a corporate vice-president of the Colgate-Palmolive Company, is married to a top executive in a conglomerate. "I was already firmly established in a career pattern when we were married," Tina says, "so my husband knew pretty much what to expect. Frankly we live by delivery. We seldom cook, and usually, when we eat at home, we have food that has already been prepared sent in. When we entertain, everything's catered. A maid who's been with me for years keeps the place clean, and since my tastes and my husband's in decorating are very different, when we disagree about the furnishings we ask a decorator to make the choice. That way we never fight over anything like the color or price of a carpet because obviously neither of us was responsible!"

Fran and Tina both feel that having a career makes their marriages more interesting for their husbands, but both add that they have friends whose experiences are different. "Some of the husbands," says Fran, "are openly hostile to the fact that their wives have careers—particularly when the wife's career is more flourishing than his. I know men who are so angry about it that they refuse to do anything at all that would be helpful or even cooperative." Obviously these marriages are in a peck of trouble.

One way to avoid *marital* tensions in households where both partners have careers is simply not to get married. This is a way chosen by a rapidly increasing number of couples: Census Bureau figures released in 1977 showed that since 1970 the number of unmarried people sharing a household with a member of the opposite sex has doubled—from 654,000 to 1.3 million. And there are undoubtedly thousands more who prefer not to tell the census takers about their living arrangement—an arrangement looked upon by President Carter and numberless others as "living in sin."

Economically the sin pays off in some ways. In addition to the old homily about two living as cheaply as one, there are tax benefits. For instance, a cohabitating couple may pay $400 less taxes on a joint income of $20,000 than a legally married pair. Usually the cohabiters get the same life insurance rates as their married friends, but they may pay higher rates for automobile and home insurance.

But coupling via cohabitation rather than marriage does not always solve the problems of career people living together and frequently creates others out there in executive country. The cohabiters quarrel about the same things married couples do: money, division of labor, infidelity, sex—not necessarily in that order. Additionally, "corporate morality" has not kept pace with the new sexual freedom. While certain industries, mainly those connected with show biz, have always done a certain amount of winking, blinking and nodding at the going mores, most corporations have a marked preference for executives who are married and presumably "settled." Maybe the marriage is as unsettling as the Civil War, but it still marks a candidate for a key job as solid and sincere—a safer bet than an unmarried in any situation, let along one who is "shacking up."

Carole (who asked me not to use her last name) was a key executive in line for a promotion in a large conglomerate, where it was understood that she would become head of a division when the chief retired. "Phil and I had been living together for five years," she said, "and our relationship was more stable than most marriages. Things have changed so much—I mean, living together has become so accepted—that I didn't dream my private life could make any difference at the office. But it did. As soon as I stopped keeping our arrangement a secret, my career took a one-hundred-and-eighty-degree turn. When the chief retired, I didn't get the job. What I did get was banishment—to an area everyone knew I hated. I knew that meant they wanted me to quit. Phil got passed up for promotion at his office, too. We're still together, but I doubt that we'll be much longer. We fight a lot now. . . ."

If you're into cohabitation, unless you and your partner are out there over the rainbow in the Sally Quinn–Ben Bradlee category, it's better not to publicize your liberated life-style. As corporations grow, they tend to grow more conservative, and while there is much talk of a relaxed outlook in the boardroom, don't count on it. A woman can get past the corporate critics as a single or a divorcée, but the company will find her more promotable if she's married or widowed. I do not suggest rushing out and getting married for the sake of a career or poisoning your husband if you can no longer stand the sight of him. But I do suggest that you keep mousy quiet at the office about any cohabitation you get involved in.

What If We Wake Up Screaming?

Married or not, career couples usually get along better when they work at jobs apart from each other. As with office romances, a quarrel that begins in bed or at breakfast can continue at the office.

For about a year I struggled to do the advertising for a chain of ultra-chic boutiques owned and operated by a couple whose relationship was more like the raid on Entebbe than a marriage. They lived in California, a fact which, for me, was fortunate by day and devastating by night. Californians tend to forget that it's three hours later in New York than it is on their own musical clocks and call up in the dead of night. So it was with "Rose" and "Elmer." He would phone me at one-thirty and say, "What's the matter with you? You sound sleepy. Well— never mind—I know you wouldn't be asleep at ten-thirty. Rose says you told her those wools I bought in Edinburgh won't sell. Now I know it's Rose who hates them because she doesn't have any taste. I just want you to tell her how wrong she is. She's on the extension. . . ."

Rose would start screaming. "Elmer says you told him my styles are 'overproduced.' *He's* the bastard who tries to make me think I'm not a designer. He says I'm just a clothes *decorator*. Tells all our friends that what Rose does is copy something great and mess it up with gook. Now he wants me to think you said it. Straighten the dumb sonofabitch out!"

I finally resigned the account one miserable morning at 5:13, New York time.

Rose and Elmer's elegant boutiques are descended from the old mom-and-pop shops—the corner grocery stores, delis, newsstands, bakeries and dry goods establishments which were operated by four hands until each child the couple produced was old enough to bring two more hands into the business. The young legs were also welcome appendages to these small enterprises and were pressed into service for trips to the post office, deliveries and other errands, since there was seldom enough money for payouts in wages.

Many of the operators of today's mom-and-pop shops aren't moms and pops at all but married couples, or cohabitants, who prefer running their own errands to looking after children. Some of them, of course, do have children and are teaching them the basics of their own businesses or crafts. In the 1960s and early 1970s many of these couples were colorful dropouts, content to earn enough money for the body-and-soul minimums—a place to flop, the fad food of the hour and "a stash of hash" (or marijuana or acid). Now ambition has set in among them, and a great many of these couples are making noises recognizable as the grunts of empire builders. Ten years ago the woman involved declared herself happy to be "the old lady" who did a large share of the fetching and toting; today she openly enjoys the role of Boss Lady.

In a North Carolina city, a couple I'll call the Vs work together during the six intense weeks when license plates are being sold in the city—and a number of weeks before and after. The license plate franchise is hers, and the location is his—a tire sales company and auto repair garage. Mrs. V. is a loud, explosive type whose bite in no way resembles her bark as she bustles about handling both customers and employees with kindness and tact. Mr. V. is quiet, low-keyed and affable but a go-getter type who arrives at work early. This permits her to finish home chores before coming in much later in her own car. They work in close quarters that are both unattractive and uncomfortable; this causes them to yell at each other, but without rancor. Since Mrs. V. is inclined to talk at top volume and say everything twice, he is not beyond shouting, "Oh, shut up!" several times a day. Friends say they get along famously at home, where there's spaciousness, beauty and all the comforts the stores offer—thanks to their interactive efforts during the license plate season which adds to the year-round income from Mr. V's garage and tire company.

The styles of living and working together are as richly varied as the couples themselves. One of the most interesting I've heard about was reported by a friend who teaches school in Kansas. The school superintendent is a man I'll call Carl Chisolm. His wife, Sally, works for him as secretary-bookkeeper-office manager. Both are in their thirties. They live across the street from the school, and at work everything is togetherness incarnate, full of interdependence and affectionate cooperation. But to keep the togetherness from getting too thick, at home they have separate bedrooms, eat few meals together and seldom go out together except to high school events. When anyone ventures a comment on the arrangement (which is a bit unusual in Kansas and in high schools anywhere), Carl only shrugs and says, "So what. We're still married. And we like it this way."

As a woman who has never married anybody, I have been pummeled since puberty with an infinite variety of questions meant to flatter, insult, needle, put down or just pry: What's a nice person like you doing single? How come you can't even get married? How can you stand being single? Aren't you lonely all by yourself? Isn't it frustrating not to have a husband? But mostly, the plain, simple interrogation: *Why aren't you married?*

My Uncle Harry, who died a bachelor at age eighty-four, had a standard answer for that which applies to my situation. Harry said, "The ones I wanted didn't want me. And the ones that did, the devil wouldn't have!"

Looking at the experiences of Karen, Joann, Fran, Tina, Carol and many another female half of the working couple, I find the following pointers very important:

1. *Don't get trapped in an effort to be all things to all people at home and the office, too.* Everybody loses—and the big loser will be you. Since serious career women are overambitious by nature, the frustration is apt to destroy you, your marriage or both.

2. *Divide responsibilities along the lines of least resistance, not tradition.* For example, if you hate running the vacuum or reprimanding the maid, let him do it while you take over something he dislikes. If you both find a chore abhorrent, take turns.

3. *Don't do anything for your husband that you can't do graciously.* Maybe he'd rather have you perform little housewifey services for him and bitch about it than suffer along without your help when you refuse, but if there's no pleasure in the effort for you, you'll feel put upon and show it.

4. *Have a firm understanding about money.* If there's a big argument about this, put the agreement in writing. Should your income surpass his, now or later, only you can decide whether to let him know about it—and how. It depends on the personalities of both parties. Some men can't take it. And some women can't either. I know of a divorce pending right now because the wife couldn't adjust to a raise that shot her salary past his.

5. *Should you move in with a dear friend or have him move into your place, keep it off the six o'clock news.* Your sophisticated friends won't be impressed one way or the other, but there are important people at your company who might make a note of it—and the note may be one that will block your plans.

18

The Mid-Life Urge

It goes without saying: The job that's hardest to get is always the first one, and the difficulty is doubled if you have been a stay-at-home wife and mother for umpteen years and have developed an itch for a career in business. There are, of course, exceptions, but you may not be one of them.

First-job difficulty is an unexpected pie in the face for young people, especially college graduates who are confident that the world is waiting for them—until they arrive at the front door. It is tougher by far for the queasy woman who wants to go back to work after years of being off the firing line—and for her friend across the street who may have spent years toiling in her own home but has never worked a day in her life beyond her own welcome mat.

Every year numberless women confront this traumatizing situation as widows, divorcées and "separateds." Additionally, there are the still-marrieds who find the family exchequer caught in a squeeze, as well as countless others who seek an outlet from boredom, a chance to develop a long-suppressed talent or escape from an empty nest that has become depressing now that the children have grown up and flown away.

Whatever the reason, a woman who has had the responsibilities of looking after a home, husband and children is likely to place a higher value on her services than management does. At the same time she is unlikely to feel happy when she is told what to do and how to do it by men who are younger than she is, women who are approximately the same age but haven't had her kind of basic and practical experience, women who are younger (regardless of training or capability) and men of any age who are obviously getting high salaries in spite of the fact that they don't know very much and don't work very hard either.

Recently, an unusually attractive woman whom I'll call Francine Rafferty described her work problems to me like this: "I was forty-six years old when I went back to business, and I just couldn't get used to being treated like dirt. At home I had prestige. My husband and children treated me with respect, and what I said went. What I say here goes, all right—in one ear and out the other. Nobody asks me what I think about anything, and if I forget and venture an opinion, they just look at me like 'Who asked *you*?' I don't like it. But that's the way it is here, and it was the only job I could get."

Back to the "Salt Mines"!

If you're a woman "of an age" going back to business or approaching it for the first time, don't expect drumrolls and a twenty-one-gun salute, but try not to feel like a helpless victim of Catch-22 either—that is, an applicant needing experience to get the job and needing the job to get the required experience. First of all, don't listen to gratuitous advice from friends. Accept all the comfort and moral support you can get from them, but don't take their amateur counsel seriously. The people who cherish you will cheer you up and on with all kinds of naive suggestions:

. . . A woman with your flair for fashion should be the buyer for the Paris salon of the local clothes emporium. (Wow! Can you pick 'em! You look like a million bucks all the time. But it so happens that the store's tacky buyer has a degree in retailing and ten years of experience, starting in the store's stock room.)

. . . A woman with your taste in decorating should be sifting through the unplundered palaces of Europe and the Orient, selecting treasures to grace the major outlets for art and antiques. (*You* could make an igloo or a Masai dung hut look super. Sure. But the buyer for your favorite furniture store has been at it since 1952 and constantly shores up his knowledge with refresher courses in art and history.)

. . . A woman with your culinary talents should be the chief exec for the town's biggest catering service or one of its superelegant restaurants. (*You* could run rings around Craig Claiborne and Julia Child—to say nothing of all those chefs with the paralyzed taste buds and recipes for instant heartburn. Maybe so. But the catering service and the restaurant your friends have in mind are probably operated by someone who studied management at Wharton, and have you ever served dinner to five hundred people in one evening?)

Your friends and relatives probably mean well and may be right about your unexploited gifts. But when it comes to marketing your talents as they apply to contemporary business, your eager loved ones just don't know what they're talking about. Jobs today require a great deal more than flair and taste, and while it is altogether true that you may do a number of things better than they're being done by the yo-yos who have them now, management isn't apt to think so. Managements place high value on successful track records and are inclined to pay heavy money only to men who brought in a beautiful "bottom line" somewhere or other. Never mind if it's fairly obvious that they could never do it again. Never mind that the final figure might have been produced in spite of them. The spoils still go to the man on the scene—or an occasional woman—when that vaunted bottom line was written.

Without recent business experience glorified by those gorgeous bottom lines, your future may seem bleak, but it needn't be. New opportunities are opening up all the time, and personnel managers who once talked only to fresh-faced youngsters are now welcoming mature women to the fold, believing them to be more settled and more serious about career commitments.

The first thing to do if you're starting out in mid-life is to take inventory: List your assets, everything you know and everything you can do really well, no matter how remote it may seem; then list your liabilities, anything that could possibly stand between you and the interesting, productive job you hope to find.

Simona McCray parlayed one of her homemaking skills into an exciting and lucrative position at CBS and, at the same time, struck a brilliant blow for the "still-marrieds" who want to work. At age forty-plus, Simona looked in her mirror and saw a singer whose educational background consisted of studies at Radcliffe, a degree from Sarah Lawrence and special training at the Mannes School of Music in Manhattan. She also had fluency in several languages learned for her anticipated career in opera. Not very promising for business, but they were what she had—in addition to an outgoing nature and infectious enthusiasm.

"I married a singer," she says, "and he was always a great deal more dedicated to the profession than I was. We toured the world together, and both of us continued to take singing lessons because in opera, continuing study is a must. When there was suddenly not enough money to pay for lessons for both of us, I deferred to him because it meant more to him than it did to me. I took up homemaking full time, but I was bored with the job

222

and wanted to earn some money, too. Since I had learned Italian, French and German to sing opera, I began giving language lessons but still didn't have enough to do to keep me occupied."

Simona's first pupil was an executive chef who wanted to speak Italian. He also needed a cook, and when he learned that she had some extraordinary gourmet skills, he employed her to delight the palates of financial tycoons in the executive dining room he presided over on Wall Street. Yes, she was a cook—the same as at home, only she got paid for it. When he became head chef at the CBS executive dining room, she went along to perform her magic for the greats in television and radio. There she began to meet important CBS people, applied for a number of jobs in the vast network and eventually got one. She is now a superstar in radio "spot sales," selling commercial time to advertisers on CBS stations all over the country without ever having to leave town.

At CBS, women are doing so well in the sales area that a member of the staff there wisecracked, "If *Death of a Salesman* were written today, it would probably be subtitled *Birth of the Saleswoman*." Seven of the eight people who sell commercial time for CBS-FM Radio are women! It should be noted, however, that in *television* sales, where the really heavy money is made, men still make up the overwhelming majority. Very few women have been admitted to this superlucrative area.

The New Frontier for Women—Guess What?

Simona is hardly typical, but her experience does indicate that some rather esoteric and unlikely skills can be door openers to a wonderful new career. It also points up a dramatic development that is taking place in business. The new frontier for women is in sales—and if you're repelled by the very thought of it, think again. Think about the women out there who are quietly earning big money, meeting important people, enjoying the world of expense accounts and credit cards that used to be the exclusive province of the male! Some of them are in their twenties and thirties, but most of the upper-bracket earners are not young anymore.

In the past women have been standoffish about going into sales, partly because of the nonglamorous image that salesmen have picked up and partly because they were unaware of the spectacular earning possibilities. The big earners have kept a very low profile, preferring not to let the competition know how well they're doing. Keeping quiet about income is always a good idea for a woman up there in the high-priced seats. Men get unreasonably upset about this—especially the ones who aren't doing as well—and go for her jugular with joyful vengeance. So do other women. But as the saying goes, most of these top performers "cry all the way to the bank."

David King, founder of a company called Careers for Women, Inc., conducts a school based on the premise that any woman who is reasonably bright and energetic should be making at least $50,000 a year, especially if she's not a late model. King's school is headquartered in New York, but he offers his course at seminars which he personally conducts in key cities around the country. There is no charge to the women King trains. He places them in high-level jobs and charges a fee to the company on a guaranteed basis. If, after six months, the company feels constrained to let one of them go, King refunds the fee. He also shows women how to set up their own businesses, to start right in as the boss.

"Instead of training women to be salespeople," King says, "we train them to be teachers—because teaching is a better word than selling. A lot of women don't want to think of themselves as salespeople and are convinced that they can't sell, but it's easy enough for them to think that what they are doing is actually teaching. We are living in an era of consumerism, which has produced a more sophisticated and wary customer. Also, since the average customer has grown up on product 'puffery,' today's salesman has a slightly negative image. It would obviously be advantageous if a company could create a less suspicious atmosphere in which to tell its sales story. The right kind of salesperson can do this; the right kind of salesperson is someone who doesn't look like a salesman; the salesperson who looks least like a salesman is a woman!"

David King goes on to say, "Men are culturally conditioned to be dishonest, whereas women are open and candid. It's refreshing. They create a different kind of climate for the buyers. Their story is heard in a less guarded atmosphere. Women seem better able to establish rapport with prospects. Women listen better and therefore take in the information that can be helpful to them in making the sale.

"While a woman in sales is no longer unique, she is still unusual and, when she contacts a prospect, is more likely to be granted an interview than her male counterpart. If she had no other advantage, she would outsell a salesman simply because of this one fact—that her sales story will be heard by more prospects."

David King clearly is talking not about behind-the-counter or door-to-door selling but about sales in stocks and bonds, insurance, television time, radio spots, newspaper and magazine space and "big ticket" items such as automobiles. Unfortunately there are still companies resistant to the idea of the new female salesperson. They stick with the time-honored salesman and are stuck with his Willie Loman-ish habit of relying on a shoeshine and smile and a hearty handshake—and all those rowdy booze-offs with the boys that run the expense account into outer space.

A couple of years ago a woman of my acquaintance saved her company from bankruptcy by invoking, as chief executive officer, a number of economy measures that included moving the annual sales meeting from the casino-hotel at a resort where it had always been held to a place in midtown Chicago where the atmosphere was all business instead of all-night gambling and drinking.

"The men were, at first, so furious that I thought I was going to be lynched!" she says. "But the purpose of the sales meeting had been defeated by its location. We threw thousands of dollars down the drain flying key people from all over the country to this glamour spot and keeping them there in sybaritic splendor, where they shot craps, drank and played golf for five days instead of concentrating on the sales plan for the coming year. In fact, the visual materials for one meeting were bumped from the company plane to make room for golf clubs! Another plane was chartered—at horrendous expense!—to take the visual aids, but they didn't arrive until the meeting was over. Everybody was too drunk to care, but the company sales figures were a sobering sight. When I took over, I changed the national sales meeting from a vacation romp to a serious business session, and the bottom line reacted accordingly. Of course, those salesmen who earned a vacation romp were rewarded with one, but the free-fun-in-the-sun for everybody was over. Some of them quit, but we didn't need those who were just there for the ride anyway. They were replaced with serious-minded men and women who appreciated the fact that the company was run on a businesslike basis."

Sales is the heart of most businesses. It offers attractive new opportunities for women, but there are reactionary companies around that still consider selling a man's job and exclude women from this vital area. Francine Rafferty (mentioned earlier) is a secretary in the home furnishings field, where she wants to move into sales. Before she was married, she worked in home furnishings for five years (as a secretary), trying all the time to get into selling and trying again when she came to work for the second time around. No dice. The home furnishings field is still an amazing male bastion in spite of the fact that its products are purchased (or passed up) by women, almost 100 percent! The men in it may point with understandable pride to the figures. It is a multi-billion-dollar industry with sales in 1976 (the last year reported) totaling $73.8 billion in the United States. Question: How much more profitable would it be, how much more comfortable and content with their surroundings would both sexes be, if women were more involved in the business that reaches into the very heart of their interests?

On the other hand, there are women who will never like selling, no matter what it's called, and will never be convinced that salesmanship is involved in every business undertaking, although this is one of life's simple truths. Everything that flourishes must be "sold" by someone at some point—whether it's a poem, a play, an ideology or an insurance policy. Women who do not like selling per se can still find interesting ways to make a living. Businessmen are beginning to realize that women can often accomplish things that men cannot, that their cultural conditioning as a simple result of gender gives them a competitive edge.

Would You Swap a New Car with This Woman?

So it is with an unusual business in California that is bound to spread across the country. In the summer of 1977 the *Wall Street Journal* ran an article about a clearing center for automobile dealers—one of the last businesses where anyone would expect to encounter women. In Bakersfield, California, there is a firm called the Dealers Exchange that arranges swaps of trucks and cars between dealerships, and all forty-one of its field representatives are women. They don't sell. They get the dealers together.

"To say that men are less capable than women at this job is a bit of an understatement," says Jean Alderson, one of the Dealers Exchange representatives. "They're totally helpless at it, bless their hearts." It seems that men are unable to cope with the impatient and sometimes abusive automobile salesmen who need a car or truck immediately for a customer who won't wait. Of the seven men hired by the exchange in recent years, two had to be fired and the other five quit in fewer than two months.

Laurel Leff, the staff reporter who wrote the article, said that the Exchange works like this:

> Let us suppose that Morey Sharkskin at Belchfire Motors has a customer who wants—insists on—a dove-gray Lincoln Mark IV, a Cartier designer model with lumbar massage seats and quad stereo. A rep for the exchange gets a panic call from Mr. Sharkskin who doesn't have the car in his lot and sees a healthy commission vanishing. The Exchange's rep scans the weekly inventory sheets from auto makers showing which dealers in their area got what, and finds an auto at Bonanza Motors that more or less meets the needs of Belchfire. The field rep then calls Bonanza to make sure the car hasn't been sold and tries to secure it for Belchfire (reminding Bonanza if necessary that it has received special favors in the past). The dealers settle the details between themselves.

The vice-president and general manager of Dealers Exchange is Claire Holmes, who is described by reporter Leff as a "slender ex-dancer" who wears crisp polka-dot dresses, speaks in the lilting inflections of a finishing-school headmistress and calls the employees "my girls," even though some are many years beyond girlhood. Leff quotes Holmes as saying that the dealers are grateful for the service because it can make them hundreds or thousands of dollars on a sale that might have been lost altogether. "When they call," says Claire Holmes, "they have customers and commissions at stake. They could be angry. They could be frantic. They are exuberant, aggressive people. It's important to talk to them with a smile in your voice." She teaches her "girls" to do exactly that, and they are said to bring their company an annual profit of $185,000 on revenues of more than $1 million.

It should be pointed out that while all forty-one representatives of the company are women, the president is a man. Since women are so well suited to the activity, it stands to reason that a business like this is a good one for a woman to stake out for herself. It should also be pointed out, however, that setting up a business like this requires more than a soothing voice, a conciliatory manner and an unflappable disposition—all excellent qualities for a woman in top management, but not enough. It requires capital, intimate knowledge of the inner workings of that particular business and a great deal of administrative expertise, too.

All over the country, women who are retiring from the housewife business are enrolling in colleges and special schools to get the training they need to excel in a given field. This is a great idea. Now that medicine, social attitudes and modern merchandising are keeping both sexes younger longer, women have a stepped-up interest in "learning and doing" outside the home. Most women of forty can't see themselves staring at daytime television for the next thirty-five years or so, even if they can afford it, and they welcome the opportunity to do something useful.

Night schools are overrun with mature women who need substantial income but find themselves unequipped to earn it. These women take the jobs they can get while preparing themselves for the jobs they want. The double schedule is tough, but those I talk to are not discouraged. Most of them say they enjoy the challenge. Linda Franklin, a young divorcée I know who has gone back to work, says, "I was getting very rusty at home, and it's good for me to do the kind of stretching I have to do now to keep a job and go to night school, too."

Here are some practical suggestions for the homemaker setting out to crack the business world:

1. *Take stock of yourself, as realistically as you possibly can.* Don't kid yourself. But don't underestimate yourself either. Make a list of all the things you do well, all the things you know a lot about and have a particular interest in, all the things you'd like to know more about, too.

2. *Study the list carefully and decide (a) what you're equipped to do right now and (b) what you'd really like to do if you could.*

3. *Make another list of everything that could stand in your way.* Include the things that apply to the (b) above.

4. *If you've let yourself go at home, recycle yourself.* If you need to lose weight, stop talking about it and do it. Extra pounds add extra years. Get professional help with your hair, makeup and clothes if you need it.

5. *Consider sales.* Insurance companies, brokerage firms, real estate companies and many others are training women to earn mind-blasting incomes. Since almost ev-

erything in life (even the loftiest idea) requires some kind of selling, rid yourself of any prejudice you may feel and think of yourself as a wealthy teacher.

6. *Define your goals, and be sure they're ambitious.* If you're going to work, you might as well make it emotionally and financially rewarding. Don't think you can't make it at your age. Your age, whatever it is, may even turn out to be an asset.

7. *Don't hesitate to go to school for any advanced or specialized studies you need to realize your goals.* There was a time when you might have felt out of place with all the youngsters in your classes, but now you'll find yourself studying beside plenty of people in your own age-group.

8. *Don't expect to be treated with the respect and deference you had at home, and don't act like an offended duchess when you're not.* Some people are abrupt (period). Don't let it upset you when you get a snappish answer. Try to keep your own good manners operative no matter how other people behave. This is especially important if you're not younger than springtime. The youngsters around you will just think you're acting "old and crotchety."

19

Your Own Damned Thing

Working for yourself is altogether different from working for somebody else. Mainly you get a harder job and a tougher boss. And you may be surprised to learn that operating your own business is not just a matter of doing "your own thing" no matter how well you may do it. It involves some rather delicate adjustments to people who are doing *their* own thing and are equally determined to do it.

Possibly you've dreamed all your life of having a corner of the business world that's yours alone, and it's only natural that you should start out to the tune of Sinatra's gold-plated recording of "I Did It My Way." It's a great song because it's everybody's dream. But it is a *dream*, for almost everybody but Ol' Blue Eyes, himself. You can set impressive policy and put the terms of that policy under glass or carve them in stone. They may look grand and make you sound like the next big dynamo. But it's more realistic to start out with a soft lead pencil and an eraser. Changes are not only necessary but healthy, and failure to make them can give your business a terminal case of the vapors.

I operate an advertising agency in Manhattan's Time/Life Building. My clients include a few people who are as sick as I am of bullshit and agree with me that it isn't the catalyst it used to be in selling goods and services. Even if it still worked, we'd walk on the other side of the street.

My first client was Stephen D'Agostino, who often goes against "conventional wisdom," believing it to be a contradiction in terms. "'Conventional wisdom,'" he says, "means general agreement, and when just about everybody thinks something, it isn't likely to be wise." Steve is head of a Manhattan supermarket chain but is no run-of-the-potato-bin grocery man. He is a literate man who does as he pleases and often delights reporters by providing them quotes outside the expected party lines. In 1977, when a television commentator interviewed him about the war between supermarkets and fast-food outlets, he opened up by mentioning that he'd had a Big Mac and a chocolate shake for lunch that day and enjoyed both enormously. This kind of honesty has endeared his stores to a sophisticated public that has long been weary of self-serving statements to the press and inflated ad claims.

For at least twenty years customers everywhere have been trying to tell everybody who sells anything that they are bored with most of the advertising that bombards them and unconvinced by the corporate chest thumps about caring and saving. I agree with their plaint and try to practice another kind of advertising.

I had collaborated with Steve on a string of successful advertising campaigns for his stores. The first was "Please Don't Kiss the Butcher," which was also the first of a long line of "Please Don't" ad themes picked up by others. We didn't mind. Advertising is a tough business, and any perspiring ad person who is stuck for a creative idea is welcome to use one of ours. I have always felt that knowing what to steal is genius, too, and only hope that anybody who makes off with a bit of my pearly prose or poesy knows how to make it work.

However, when Mr. Whipple popped up on television every hour or so, admonishing the customers not to squeeze his toilet tissue, we moved along to another theme—"If There's No D'Agostino Near You, Take a Taxi." That one was so well received that we shifted gears and went into "If There's No D'Agostino Near You —Move," with illustrations by cartoonist Marvin Glass.

Life in the Supermarket Rafters

My first office was in the loft of a D'Agostino super-market at Eighty-fifth Street and Lexington Avenue, thirty to forty blocks north of midtown Manhattan. The location was terrible, but the price was right. It was free. And it gave me the perfect vantage point to learn about the inner workings of supermarkets, which are the sales focus of thousands of today's products.

Few things in life are as exhilarating as the first glorious weeks in your own business—that easy, breezy time before reality sets in. Naming the place is step one. I know people who have given more thought to naming a business than meeting the payroll. These are mostly people who started out in the era of cutesy names when advertising agencies and related firms greeted the world with some wondrously lighthearted corporate monikers meant to reflect creativity. The trouble with a fanciful name is that a prospective client hunting Gloria Cheltingham may have a hard time finding her if she has named her company The Brain Strain. I decided to use my own name, and unless yours has somehow become Mudd, I heartily recommend that you use it when you go into business for yourself. People can at least find you in the phone book, and you may even want to talk to some of them.

Step two is decorating. Since I was located in a su-permarket loft, I opted for bright colors and very modern decor—a white fur rug (which I quickly abandoned) and a stainless-steel-and-glass desk, echoed by a stainless-steel-and-marble arc lamp which I still have. Another client, who imports the leather used in the interiors of the

Rolls-Royce, wanted to dramatize the leather's availability in fifty-two colors, so I had a chaise longue made up using all of them. (He supplied the custom-dyed leather for free, and I paid for the chaise.) A trompe l'oeil grandfather clock was painted on the wall around an antique clock face, flanked by a collection of French posters. The overall effect was startling, to say the least. People who struggled up the steps to see me, picking their way past crates of produce and cases of Budweiser, were astonished by what they found at the top of the stairs.

Since there was room in the place for only me and one visitor (maybe two small ones), I had no help and in the first weeks had no need for any. I was in the ideal spot to learn more about the supermarket business and had few distractions.

There were other splendid advantages, not the least of which was that I could look through the air ducts and watch customers shoplifting on the selling floor below. My favorite shoplifter was an ancient crone who lightfingered the merchandise selectively. She would root through all the steaks in the meat case, demolishing the meticulous symmetry of the butcher's painstaking display. Finally selecting a sirloin that would have seemed pretentious to Henry VIII, she would take it to the front of the store, examine it in the glare of the daylight and, ceremoniously stuffing it into the recesses of her homemade reticule, sail grandly past the checkout stand without paying. Sometimes, after examining the meat in the daylight, she would shrug, march back to the meat case and toss it arrogantly onto the packages she had jumbled. On these occasions the store manager would look heavenward, unable to believe that anyone had found such a fine cut of beef not good enough to steal.

"Don't you ever do anything about her?" I asked the manager one day.

"Don't I ever do *what* about her?" he replied. "An

eighty-five-year-old woman? You think maybe I should call a cop and get her thrown into the slammer? Mr. D'Agostino would kill me—if I didn't kill myself first."

The rent was indeed right, but as previously mentioned, the location was terrible. A few other accounts came over the transom, and these required me to make several trips a day to the midtown area. My apartment is at the wrong end of Fifth Avenue, between Eighth and Ninth Streets. When you live that far downtown, and have an office that far uptown and clients in the middle, travel back and forth in New York traffic can swallow the days up whole. There were times struggling back and forth in taxis, or a combination of subways and buses, when I thought I had died and gone to hell and was doing penance for past transgressions.

To cope with the problem, I had to learn how to operate out of a Dag Bag, the famous D'Agostino shopping bag we had designed. The Dag Bag had providentially become a status symbol when models everywhere started carrying their extra shoes and makeup in it. (The bag has been seen in the Tokyo airport, on the streets of Paris, London and Moscow and on flights of most of the major airlines.) In mine, I carried advertising layouts mixed in with makeup, shoes, various other articles of clothing, media schedules and telephone numbers—dozens of telephone numbers to return the calls intercepted by the answering service I had in lieu of an office staff.

The best office-away-from-the-office in New York is the Waldorf. It has the best public john in town—spacious, gracious and so altogether "nice" that it seems to be a breach of civilized human behavior to exercise a bodily function there. The plumbing is not walled off by those tacky half-doored stalls that are in the ladies' rooms of most public facilities. The attendant is deliriously grateful for a dollar tip and acts as if you had presented her with a deed to a theater-district parking lot. She ushers you into a large room with a whole door on it. It is equipped with all the propr plumbing plus makeup lights that cheer you up by making you look better than you have any right to expect. You can write a letter, make notes and collect your thoughts in the large foyer. And you leave feeling the way people who live by tips should make you feel—supremely confident—rather than with a gnawing notion that you've been victimized by the necessity to resort to public facilities.

The Waldorf also has a long lineup of telephones for the use of passersby and a restaurant (Peacock Alley) where you can talk to clients without being overheard by their competitors and your own because most of the people there are visitors from places like Toledo, Birmingham and Detroit. Great as the Waldorf is for office uses, I had to turn to the Plaza for a free conference room. This was not my discovery but that of Jane Brown, who at the time was fashion director for Sears and is now a designer of children's clothing. Jane and Alice Reichenbach, who was Sears' assistant publicity director, wanted to see a makeup and fashion promotion that had been put together for me by Dotti Sherman. Among other things, Dotti had designed exercise suits using an original tiger print she had created. We had lunch at the Plaza, and I had the samples and sketches with me—in a Dag Bag. We could hardly spread all these out in the Edwardian Room, so Jane whistled the bell captain up and tipped him handsomely enough to get us escorted into the Persian Room, which was closed by day, coming to life at the time as a supper club for night people. Even with the cloths off the tables, the Persian Room made an impressive conference room, and I pressed it into service for presentation purposes on many subsequent occasions.

Finally, I had to give up and take midtown office space, although it caused me emotional pain that was almost physical, to leave my office in the D'Agostino loft. I missed that eighty-five-year-old selective shoplifter, the trompe l'oeil clock and the skylight that canopied the whole place. But reality was setting in fast, and I realized my need for more formalized space. I moved to East Fifty-fifth Street, taking a small suite in a building where Janis Joplin was headquartered with a company called The Cheap Thrills, another bit of creative naming which has been nowhere more prevalent than in the recording business, where it somehow seems to fit. Janis was a spectacular performer on and off the stage, and when she arrived in the building in a flurry of feathers and jingle of bells, it was the best show in town. Offices emptied so everybody could watch.

One thing that brought me out of the D'Agostino rafters was the J. C. Penney Company which had opened up a division called The Treasury. The Penney organization is an authentic hunk of Americana operating more than 2400 stores in cities, towns and whistle stops from Maine to Hawaii, Puerto Rico to Alaska—catnip to an advertising person genuinely interested in reactions out there in the so-called hinterlands.

The Treasury Division's stores were conceived as experimental laboratories testing new methods in every phase of retail operation, from lighting and fixturing to merchandising and marketing. I felt duly catnipped at being recruited to work on the advertising with The Treasury's superwoman, June Thursh, advertising and sales promotion director of the division.

Our first assignment was to create an "image" for the Treasury stores, along with introductory advertising campaigns for them in Atlanta, Memphis, Miami and Los Angeles. Interestingly, the advertising we did that evoked the most positive responses from the store managers (all men) was a jingle with the recurring refrain "The Treasury Is Here to Save You!" sung by a heavy male chorus.

Of course, the saving referred to was money, but one of the happy Penney men finally expressed the emotion that accounted for the jingle's appeal to the whole group: "Sounds like the men are really rescuing the ladies—and I like that!" Providentially nobody mentioned the Sabine women.

Yet another early client of mine was Lamston's, the New York chain of five-and-dime stores where such celebrities as Ethel Merman, Jackie O. and a few Rockefellers rub elbows with the city's melting-pot population to buy life's little necessities. Quick! Where in a town like this can you grab a sink stopper? A spool of thread? A screwdriver! A safety pin? Burton Adelman, the chain's president, and Fred Marks, chairman, tell New Yorkers where on television and radio and in the local newspapers, but not often enough to suit an ad woman. Still, who am I to quarrel with a management that's got the redoubtable Ms. Merman offstage? Needless to say, she is in no need of rescue.

It's No Fun to Fail—Even When You're "Just a Girl"

Being in business for one's self is more difficult for a woman than it is for a man. Although things are changing, they are not changing as fast as we would like to believe, and women still are not really expected to make it. Nor is it considered very important if we don't. The fact that failure is as rattling and disappointing to most women as it is to most men seems to be a new idea, something that just blew into town with the revolution.

A man is, and always has been, expected to succeed —to provide well for the needs of his family, to be a source of pride to his wife and children, a man to be reckoned with by other men and to be kept up with by the neighbors. When he falls on his face or any other part of his anatomy, it's a personal earthquake, and he is shaken further by the realization that he has become an embarrassment to just about everybody. Old friends avoid him, not so much because they're afraid of being hit for a loan but because they simply don't know what to say to him. How do you talk to a man who can't get it together? Most people just don't have the poise to cope with male failure.

On the other hand, nobody expects a woman to succeed in the business world. If she makes any kind of showing at all, it is looked upon as a bona fide miracle, and should she fail, it won't make much difference to anybody but her. The audience reaction will be much the same as when a chimp falls off a bicycle. The remarkable part is that she could get on the thing and ride it at all.

Men's reluctance to take a woman in business seriously is one of the disadvantages she must overcome, but in the new power game it becomes a disadvantage with a solid-gold lining. While the men are watching each other like so many hypersuspicious hawks, the rise of a smart woman can go virtually unobserved—until the announcement is made that the promotion they were slicing each other's throats to get has gone to the only available candidate whose throat remains intact.

A woman I know in the textile industry recently won a corporate vice-presidency that half a dozen men were battling one another to get. They all had been so damaged by the infighting that each man's capabilities had been laid open to serious questioning. In their zeal to expose their opponents' weaknesses, all candidates for the office had cut one another out of the running. A. was involved in a nasty divorce scandal; B. got loaded every day at lunch and often reeked of scotch *before* lunch; C. had an uncontrollable temper and not only made the good secretaries quit but had recently alienated a customer (whose temper was just as bad); D. was careless about details and weak on follow-through; E. was up to his eyeballs in debt, and collectors were beginning to show up at the office. Only the woman had no unrevealed flaws of character or performance, because the men competing for the post had not bothered to ferret them out and see to it that the brass got the word. They had dismissed her as a serious contender. She got the job!

For all management knows, she may be at the brink of divorcing her husband, have a desk full of kitchen whiskey and unpaid bills, the disposition of a wounded rhino, and a slapdash approach to everything, personal and professional. She doesn't. But if she did, none of it would have been dug out and dropped around top management, where the bosses would be sure to share the discovery. The men she jumped over didn't recognize her potential because she was, after all, "just a girl."

Having the freedom to fail is a formidable luxury. It lets you take some chances that others wouldn't dare, to go on the high trapeze without a net. As a woman you can afford to risk defeat, because when nobody expects you to win, a loss or two is hardly noticed. Any little victory, by contrast, brings everybody to his or her feet—if not to cheer, at least to see what happened. And how.

According to the figures released in 1977 by the U.S. Department of Commerce, women own 5 percent of the businesses in this country but these account for less than .3 percent of all gross receipts. The department has no recent figures on the number of business failures recorded among women owners, but most of the firms operated by females are small, like my own. Still, more and more women are electing to form their own companies because this is one of the few ways they can earn a substantial income, keep an agreeable part of it and enjoy a certain amount of job security.

One of the moldiest jokes around concerns women's insistence on always having the last word. I think the main reason we go into business for ourselves is that with rare exceptions, it's about the only way for a woman to get the first word—to set policy and make the big decisions about what the company is to be, what it is to do and who is going to be responsible for what. It is deeply satisfying to know that while the buck stops *here,* you are the one who can stop it even before it gets here.

Recently someone on a panel show asked me where is the first place a woman should look for help in setting up her own business. I immediately said, "St. Patrick's Cathedral!" But I do have some other suggestions, and here they are:

1. *Find a friend at the bank. You're going to need one.* Although the law is supposed to guarantee equal opportunity in lending, that doesn't mean you'll have immediate access to the money you need when you need it, unless at least one pair of those beady eyes at the bank looks upon you with confidence.

2. *Get an accountant who understands the kind of business you're in.* He or she may be one of the nation's great experts in dealing with the financial problems of people who manufacture rivets, but if you're going into film production, he or she won't be the kind of help you need.

3. *Guard your credit rating with your life.* Women, fair or not, are considered poorer credit risks than men, so be extra-careful with bill payments, especially in the first two years.

4. *Do not overextend your financial or physical commitments at any stage.* Of course, you want to look rich and famous. Of course, you want the world to be impressed with what you're doing. Just don't overdo it.

5. *Be sure to have enough business lined up to keep you afloat for at least a year.* I was extremely lucky to have a loyal client who was willing to give me his ac-

count and office space while I got my bearings. Running a small business is a lot like flying a small plane. You're always looking for a place to land in case the engine konks out. What if your number one customer steps in a manhole?

6. *Don't carry on and on about how well you're doing.* This will cause people of both sexes to look upon you with jealousy and your business in a covetous manner. You can appear confident without being boastful.

6. *Try not to panic when things go wrong.* The fact that the engine has missed a few beats doesn't mean that it's konked out. It only means that you should be extraordinarily alert and attentive. Above all, keep your cool and a confident facade. Nobody wants to do business with a person who looks and acts like a loser.

20

Where Do We Go from Here?

God knew what He was doing when He made two sexes, and the fact that we have not been able to work out the male-female problems at the office means only that we have been reluctant, maybe frightened, to break another pattern of the past that is so dearly and warmly familiar. Sexual differences, after all, have been just about the last things we could count on to remain the same in a world that is changing too fast for anybody's comfort or even comprehension.

Bernice Fitz-Gibbon, who was perhaps the first great Boss Lady in the advertising business, used to say that women have always been welcome at the office—to sharpen the pencils, type the swill and fetch and tote for the men. "The trouble started when they began moving into the corner offices and running things," she said. "That was when women became a threatening invasion, rather than a welcome addition." Fitz, who had more strength and courage than most bosses of either sex, who would hire nobody to work for her in any capacity unless he or she had a college degree and was also a Phi Beta Kappa, was speaking twenty years ago, but her forthright observations are paraphrased by many an executive woman today.

"The men at my company loved me when I was a secretary," says Bonni Q. "But when I finally worked my way into management, the men who used to outrank me began to resent me. When I was first promoted, one of them even had the gall to ask me if I didn't realize I was taking a job away from some man who has a family to support. He doesn't know who I have to support, and I'm not going to tell him. . . ."

Bonni's experience is not unique. Openly or covertly men remain hostile to women in executive roles. The new laws and social pressures have improved career opportunities for women, but they have not altered the basic attitudes about the human structure of businesses—who does what to whom and for how much.

Women's most dramatic progress has occurred outside the core activity of planning, manufacturing and marketing and has taken place largely in peripheral areas, where they are highly visible but not deeply involved in the big stuff. Again relegated to jobs kissed off as "woman's work." And again at "good pay—for a woman."

In May 1977 *Money* magazine reported that in 1975, the latest year for which figures were then available, the median salary for women working full time was $7,504 compared with $12,758 for men—meaning that women earned only 59 percent of what the men did. Some of the earnings differential may certainly be attributed to the large numbers of women pouring into the work force at entry-level jobs. But the Bureau of Labor Statistics fingers sexual discrimination (the cruelest kind!) as the root cause, in spite of all the antidiscrimination laws that were passed and loudly touted in the 1960s.

Rachel Lavoie, author of the *Money* article, drew this bead on the female condition in business:

A woman who hits the heights in a male-dominated profession is just as likely to be labeled a token as a trailblazer. For every career success story, there is an equal and opposite tale of woe. When a company with one female and 37 male vice presidents appoints two more women to that post, optimists say that the number of women vice presidents increased by 200%, pessimists that only 7½% of the vice presidents are women. In short, the situation of women workers today depends a lot on how you look at it. . . .

The women's revolution has spawned an interesting mix of positive and negative viewpoints. There are those who see it as a boon to womankind and the world, and others who see it as a venomous social evil or, at best, a comedy of errors. Consequently, young women starting to work today tend to view business as a male chauvinist pigsty that stinks to high hell or as a pretty pink playpen that is theirs for the taking. Of course, neither of these images is altogether true or altogether false, but just try to tell that to the men and women who have made up their minds (as so many of them have—in concrete!).

The worst thing that can be said about the revolution is that it has polarized the sexes, setting men and women who used to be reasonable human beings against each other, slashing away at each other's bulging jugulars. The second worst thing is that it has polarized women whose opinions differ, turning the organizations meant to promote female status into tragicomic shambles.

Erica Jong, the writer who has been mistaken for a feminist but may be the only genuine humanist involved in the whole sexual hoo-ha, recently wrote this in an article in *Newsweek:*

> . . . if male criticism was all we had to fear, we'd be well off indeed. Every woman who has excelled in her field knows that the bitterest experience of all is the lack of support, the envy, the bitterness we frequently get from our female colleagues. We are hard on ourselves and hard on each other. We have too little charity for each other's work, and are too apt to let the male establishment pit us against each other—token woman against token woman. If the

men just stand back and let us, we will certainly destroy each other (and our own movements) quite as efficiently as our male detractors would. More efficiently, perhaps—because we know our own weaknesses so well.

Women crave approval and support so deeply that it is doubly hard for us when it is withheld. And women not only withhold support from other women, they openly attack.

Critical though it is of women, that does sound feminist, doesn't it? But hear this, from the same Jong musings:

I . . . persist in believing that love can have an existence apart from illusion and oppression, that men and women can be friends rather than enemies, brothers and sisters rather than political sparring partners, sexual slaves, mutual oppressors, participants in a sexual suicide pact.

Erica Jong, as always, speaks from a platform of humanity and fairness. But for the moment let's leave humanity and fairness out of it and look at the matter cold-eyed, only in terms of money—which, apparently, is the medium of communication most people understand instantly, if not best. From that perspective, we have to admit that billions of dollars are flushed into the sewer system every year because the gifts and intellect of a whole sex are underused when they are not passed over or passed up. Some effort at last is being made to use them effectively, but the effort is slowed by envious women and resentful men standing on old-fashioned ceremony and crumbling ground.

Tradition, as the saying goes, dies hard. The tradition of male and female roles in business may die with the loudest screams and hardest kicks of all, but the life-sustaining systems *are* being unplugged. Just don't expect to hear any serious death rattling soon.

A lot of women, fired up by media reports on the new feminism and the changes it has brought about in business, are charging into jobs, booted and spurred, ready to take their "rightful places" in the upper reaches of the executive echelon. Still others, intoxicated by the same rush of rhetoric, are taking aggressive new stances in jobs they've had for years, expecting to get hefty promotions and salary increases as an automatic offshoot of the current push for equality.

But it just doesn't happen that way. When the pressure first went on, a few corporations did panic and slip a woman here and there into a high-salaried spot with an impressive title. But getting a meaningful executive position isn't easy—for anybody. It is an enormously difficult and demanding challenge for a man. And liberation notwithstanding, it is many times more so for any woman.

The belligerent or "ballsy" women who march in with a chip on the shoulder as big as the Ritz are in for a quick slap-down because the shot callers in management seldom take kindly to any belligerence other than their own, in either sex. The ability to get along with people is highly prized by corporate America and is looked upon as a supreme quality of leadership. Self-confidence, yes. Assertiveness, yes. Decisiveness, yes. "I-can-lick-any-guy-on-the-premises!"—out!

This brings on my final list of suggestions:

1. *Don't try to be one of the boys*. Even though you're the Boss Lady, you just aren't one of them, and there are places besides the gentlemen's urinal where you won't be welcome. Think about the places in your own life where *they* aren't welcome, and smile sincerely when you urge them to run along without you. (Of course, they invited you. You're the boss. So you're smart enough

248

to know when to decline.) In other words, stay out of the office crap game.

2. *Try to understand male bonding.* It happens all over the animal kingdom, and if men prefer to act like a pack of baboons, let them!

3. *Don't fall for a male sob story.* Weak men often appeal to the maternal instincts of strong women by spilling out the fascinating story of their problems at home. These are the men who put pictures of hollow-eyed little children on their desks, thinking no Boss Lady could be so heartless as to fire the father of this wan brood. If you do have to fire such a devoted dad, borrow some pictures of hollow-eyed little children for your own desk when you do it—and remember that you're giving him a chance to get a job where he can be effective enough to fatten up the tribe.

4. *Give the other women in your outfit a break.* Having another successful woman around (or three or four or more) will not diminish your own stature but strengthen it. Actually you're less vulnerable when you're *not* the only woman.

5. *Do not assign jobs on a gender basis.* Capability is the only realistic yardstick to use, ever, and if a woman on the premises can drive a tractor-trailer better than anybody else or a man can make the best coffee, don't just let them—insist on it!

Today's beleaguered business community needs all the help it can get, and men and women need each other there as well as everywhere else. It is to be hoped that we really are gaining fresh insights into each other's heads, and it's even encouraging to know that more companies are actively pretending. Twenty years ago most managements didn't bother.

In the end women will make it in business because their brains and hearts and guts are needed there—and because they have learned what and when and how to contribute while men (and other women) are getting used to the idea.

Gender discrimination is the last form of prejudice that is professionally and socially acceptable. Perhaps it is dying hardest because it is dying last, but this, too, shall pass.

Index

AWNY (Advertising Women of New York), 188, 189, 191–192, 195–96, 200, 202

Adams, Leon D., 165

Adelman, Burton, 239

Advertising Age, 201

Advertising Women of New York (AWNY), 188, 189, 191–92, 195–96, 200, 202

age, questions about, 171–73, 177

airplanes, fear of, 144–46

alcohol, effects of, 155, 163–67

alcoholism, 154, 162–63

Alderson, Jean, 228

Allen, Marcia, 202

American Academy of Psychoanalysis, 104

American Advertising Federation, 194, 195, 200

American Veterinary Medicine Assn., 33

Anderson, David, 210–11

appearance, personal, 55–60
of executive women, 69

appreciation, expression of, 199

authority, *see* power

Bane, Mary Jo, 205

Bartos, Rena, 202

Bassford, Suzanne, 37

behavior stereotypes, 11–12, 104–06, 118–21

Bentley, Helen Delich, 135–36

Boss Lady, 21–22, 53–54, 94–101
manner, personal, 68–69
sex life of, 183–86
types of, 94–98, 99–100

bosses, 11–14

Bown, Jane, 237

bralessness, 57–58

Brown, Helen Gurley, 175, 182–83

Brown University Club, 138

Burnett, Carol, 175

business failures, 241

business trips, 140–53

CBS office decor, 64

cab drivers, women as, 25–26

Cantlon, Joe, 35

careers for women:
choice of, 25, 40–41
mistakes, 42
future of, 244–50
guidelines to success, 22, 40–42, 53–54, 69–70, 80, 106–07, 116–17, 128–29, 139, 152–53, 187, 200–201, 206–07, 218, 230–231, 242–43, 248–49

careers for women: (*cont.*)
  income statistics, 208–09, 245
  marriage and, 208–18
  in mid-life, 219–31
  opportunities offered by
      colleges, 33–34
  planning of, 40–42
  success in, 43–54
  training for, 33–34, 41
Careers For Women, Inc., 224
Carter, John Mack, 50
Chamberlain, Joan, 40
clubs, professional, 188–201
cohabitation vs. marriage, 213–214
colleges, career opportunities
      offered by, 33–34
comments, personal, 60
Commonsense Book of Drinking, The, Adams, 165
competitiveness, 48–51
conversation, 118–129
corporations, response to EEO, 18–20
Creel, Jane, 202

Dag Bags, 236
D'Agostino, Stephen, 232–33
D'Agostino Supermarkets, 233–236
Daily Enterprise, McComb, Miss., 34–36
Dealers Exchange, 228–29
decor of offices, 64–67, 70
designers, men as, 20–21
discrimination against women, 204
Dodge, Kay, 51
double standards:
  drinking habits, 155–56, 159, 162–63, 166
  emotional behavior, 105–06
  language, 135–37

in professional organizations, 191
  public speaking, 198
  punctuality, 142, 152
  questions, personal, 171
draft laws for women, 204
dress, style of, 55–60, 69
drinking habits, 154–70
drivers, women as, 25–26

EEO (Equal Employment
      Opportunity), responses to, 18–20
ERA (Equal Rights Amendment), 202–07
Edwards, Edwin, 73
Ellard, Roscoe, 32–33
Emmerich, Lyda Will, 34–35
Emmerich, Oliver, 34–35
emotional behavior, 104–07
employees:
  undesirable types, 98–99
  women as, 48
employers, women as, 93–101
Enoki, Mrs. Misako, 149
Equal Employment Opportunity
      (EEO), responses to, 18–20
Equal Rights Amendment
      (ERA), 202–07
etiquette, business, 130–39, 156–57, 199

failure, 239–42
  of businesses, 241
  fear of, 51–52, 53
Fallone, Norbert, 38
Family Circle, 205
family life, 205–06
  of working women, 208–18
fathers, career women
      influenced by, 27
Feld, Irvin, 58

Feld, Mick, 145
femininity, maintenance of, 22
feminist movement, 73–74
Fielding, Beth, 147
fired, what to do when, 90–92
firing practices, 81, 83–92
Fitz-Gibbon, Bernice, 244
flying, fear of, 144–46, 152
four-letter words, 135–38, 139
Foxworth, Jo:
    advertising agency of, 232–38
    birthplace of, 26
    childhood and youth, 28–29,
        48–50, 101–03
    educational background, 15,
        29–33
    father of, 11–12, 27–28, 101–
        103, 119–20
    first job, 15
    journalistic career, 34–37
    mother of, 13–14, 27–28,
        101–03
    retailing experience, 36–37
Franklin, Linda, 230
Fredericks, Christine, 191–92
Freed, Joan, 132

Glass, Marvin, 233–34
glass arm, 96
Glory and the Dream, The,
    Manchester, 73
Gone With the Wind, 45
Good Housekeeping, 50
Gossage, Howard, 65
Gottschalk, Earl C., Jr., 205
Gray, Ed., 126–27
Greenberg, Leon A., 163–64
Greenwich Village Chamber of
    Commerce, 196
Gregg, Dorothy, 68

hangovers, 166–67, 169–70
Hennig, Margaret, 17

Hilton Hotels, advertising cam-
    paign for, 51–53
Hinson, Clifton, 49
hiring, 81–83, 106
    of secretaries, 116
Hogan, Joan, 202
Holmes, Claire, 229
hotel rooms for women, 52–53
Hunter, Barbara, 202–03
husbands and careers, 208–18
Hyde, Anne, 82

IBM, dress code at, 56–57
influence as alternative to
    power, 77–79
Inouye, David, 110

Japan, travel in, 148–52
Japanese businessmen, 148–52
Jardim, Anne, 17
job, loss of, 90–92
Johnston, E. K., 30
Johnston, Russ, 51–52
Jones, Janet, 82
Jong, Erica, 246–47
Jonny Mop, 22
Joplin, Janis, 288
jug, how to drink from, 31

Kennington's Department Store,
    36–37
King, David, 225
Korda, Michael, 43

Lady Hilton Rooms, 52–53
Lamston's, 239
language, offensive, 135–38, 139
    See also speech patterns
Lavoie, Rachel, 245–46
Lee, Gypsy Rose, 58
Leff, Laurel, 228–29
liquor laws, 158
listening, 121–24

losing, psychology of, 44–45
loss of job, 90–92
Louisville, Ky., 38

McCann-Erickson, 51
McComb, Miss., 34–35
McCray, Simona, 222–23
McDavid, O. C., 35
male bonding, 249
Management Woman, 82
Managerial Woman, The,
    Hennig & Jardim, 17
Manchester, William, 73
manner, personal, 22, 68–69, 70
manners, *see* etiquette
Mansfield, Ohio, 199–200
marital status, personal ques-
    tions about, 173–74
Marks, Fred, 239
Marone, Mario, 131
marriage and career, 208–18
    cohabitation, 213–14
    statistics, 208–09, 213
Martin, Patricia, 194
mathematicians, women as, 33–
    34
Mead, Margaret, 185–86
Middlebrook, Jean, 193
mid-life career, 219–31
military service for women, 204
Miller, Wallace Walton, 62–63
Mississippi State College for
    Women, 29
Mississippi University for
    Women, 29, 33
Money, 245–46
Myers, Eddie, 35
Myers, Suellen, 125–26

name-calling, 78–79
National Council of Women, 24
Newsweek, 17, 208–09, 246–47

Nine Commandments for
    Women in Business, 195–
    196
Nordin, Colleen, 37

objectives of women, 24–25
obscenities, 135–38
office decor, 64–67, 70
organizations, professional,
    188–201
outplacement, 90

patience, 151–52
Paulsen, Joann, 211
Penney, J. C., Company, 238
personal comments, 60
personal questions, 171–77
personal sacrifices, 54
Philadelphia, Pa., 39
Pistone, Frank, 99
Plaza Hotel, 237
political issues, 206–07
Power!, Korda, 65
power:
    desire for, 71–75
    tactics of, 75–76
    use of, 77–80, 100
product development, 21
professional organizations, 188–
    201
public speaking, 195–200
punctuality, 32–33, 142–43, 152
purchasing power of women,
    20–21

questions, personal, 171–77

Ramey, Estelle, 50
Reichenbach, Alice, 237
résumés, 91–92
Rhoads, Geraldine, 23–24
Rindlaub, Jean, 202–03
Roby, Vic, 29
Rodgers, Dorothy, 22

roles, sex identified, 45–47
Rooney, Michael, 211
Russell, Kathy, 160–61

sacrifices, personal, 54
salary, 208–09, 245
  questions about, 175–76
sales, careers in, 223–27
Sames, Suzanne, 37
Santi, Tina, 212
Schaufler, Flora, 26
Schlafly, Phyllis, 203–04
secretaries, 108–17
self-employment, 232–39, 242–243
Sex and the Office, Brown, 182
Sex and the Single Girl, Brown, 182
sex life:
  in business relations, 178–87
  questions about, 174–75, 177
sex roles, development of, 45–46
Shaver, Betty, 95–96
Sherman, Dotti, 237
Shiseido Cosmetics America, Inc., 148–52
shoptalk, excessive, 127–28
showcase jobs for women, 19–20
Simmons, Jill, 65–66
Sledge, Kev, 160
speech patterns, 61–63, 70
  See also language, offensive
style:
  of dress, 55–60, 69
  of office decor, 64–67, 70
  personal manner, 68, 70
  of speech, 61–63, 70
success in business, 43–54
  fear of, 46–47, 53
  psychology of, 43–44
Symonds, Alexandra, 104–05

talkativeness, 118–21, 128–29
taxi drivers, women as, 25–26
thank you notes, 199
Thursh, June, 33–34, 238
toilets, public, 204
training for careers, 33–34, 41
travel, business, 140–53
Treasury, The, division of J. C. Penney Co., 238
trips, business, 140–53
Tylertown, Miss., 26
Twain, Mark, 137

University of Missouri, 30–32

veterinarians, women as, 33
voices, female, 125–26, 129
volunteer work, 188–201

Waldorf Hotel, 236–37
Wall Street Journal, 227–28
Wallace, Delight, 61
Wilburn, Ted, 87
Williams, Jennie, 49
Williams, Johnny, 35
winning, psychology of, 43–44
Woman's Day, 23–24
women:
  age of, questions about, 171–173, 177
  behavior stereotypes of, 104–106, 118–21
  careers for, *see* careers for women
  competitiveness of, 48–51
  discrimination against, 204
  drinking habits of, 154–70
  as drivers, 25–26
  as employees, 48
  as employers, 93–101
  feminist movement, 73–74
  firing of, 90

women: (cont.)
  marital status, questions about, 173–74
  mid-life careers for, 219–31
  objectives of, 24–25
  personal questions, 171–77
  purchasing power of, 20–21
  salary, questions about, 175–176
  self-evaluation, 46–47
  sex life, questions about, 174–75, 177
  success of in business, 43–54
  successful:
    characteristics, 68–69
    dress, 55–60
  personal manner, 68–69
  personal qualities, 79
  use of power by, 77–80
  working, statistics, 17, 208–09
Women In Passage, *Good Housekeeping,* 50
Women's Advertising Club of Chicago, 193
Women's National Republican Club, 138
Worden, Karen, 210–11
working women:
  statistics, 17, 208–09
  family life of, 205–06, 208–218
writer's block, 96